D0529236

MAKING YOUR MARK IN MUSIC

music **PRO**
guides

MAKING
YOUR MARK
IN MUSIC
STAGE PERFORMANCE
SECRETS

BEHIND THE SCENES OF ARTIST DEVELOPMENT

ANIKA PARIS

AN IMPRINT OF HAL LEONARD CORPORATION

Copyright © 2011 by Anika Paris

Published in 2011 by Hal Leonard Books
An Imprint of Hal Leonard Corporation
7777 West Bluemound Road
Milwaukee, WI 53213

Trade Book Division Editorial Offices
33 Plymouth St., Montclair, NJ 07042

Permissions can be found on page 145, which constitutes an extension of this copyright page.

Printed in the United States of America

Book design by Michael Kellner

Library of Congress Cataloging-in-Publication Data

Paris, Anika.
 Making your mark in music: stage performance secrets / Anika Paris.
     p. cm.
 ISBN 978-1-61774-227-9 (pbk.)
 1. Music–Vocational guidance. 2. Music–Performance. I. Title.
 ML3795.P34 2011
 781.4'3-dc23
                          2011026681

www.halleonard.com

To all who gave me music:
my family,
my teachers,
my colleagues,
my students,
and
my Dean

CONTENTS

PREFACE   ix

PART I: FROM THE INSIDE OUT

CHAPTER 1
Finding You: Capturing What Is Already There   3

CHAPTER 2
Bridging the Gap Between Audience and Stage: Casting Yourself   13

CHAPTER 3
Three Points of View: Your Lyric Is Your Conversation   35

CHAPTER 4
Using the Chakras: Pairing the Physical and the Emotional   43

PART II: DRESS REHEARSAL

CHAPTER 5
Designing Your Set: What Do Your Songs Say About You?   53

CHAPTER 6
Between the Music: Stories and Anecdotes   63

CHAPTER 7
Finding Your Fashion Muse: Shopping in Your Closet   69

CHAPTER 8
Designing a Signature Sound: Your Band and You   81

CHAPTER 9
Technically Speaking: Things Every Singer Should Know   85

PART III: LIGHTS, CAMERA, ACTION!

CHAPTER 10
The Camera Versus the Stage: Big or Small or No One at All   99

CHAPTER 11
The Interview: Tips on How to Keep Us Tuned In   103

PART IV: THE INDUSTRY

CHAPTER 12
Behind the Desk: An A&R's Take on It All   113

PART V: PUTTING IT ALL TOGETHER

CHAPTER 13
Following Your Journey: Summing Up   127

ACKNOWLEDGMENTS   135
APPENDIX A   137
APPENDIX B   141
INDEX   147

NOTE

BONUS: Techniques from chapters 3, 4, 6, and 9 are included on the DVD that comes with this book. You can see examples of before and after (with the interview, the musical performance, and the art of conversation that you will create for yourself), and how applying my unique techniques will enhance your performance.

PREFACE

It was a Saturday morning in September, and the rain was pouring down outside my Greenwich Village apartment. I was subletting the place from my parents' best friend, renowned composer, conductor, and musician David Amram, and paying only $100.00 a month. I would sleep in the loft and wake up every morning to practice the baby grand piano in the middle of the living room. I was in my own little heaven. The neighbors, on the other hand, were probably going crazy hearing the same songs over and over again, accompanied by children playing at recess in PS 41's playground, the courtyard our tenement apartment overlooked. My brother Paul Peress and I had formed a band, Double Exposure, and we had just booked our first gig at The Bitter End. I had played a few talent shows, in living rooms for all my friends and family, and even recorded demos in the studio. But, this was my first real show and our New York City debut, with a guest list of over one hundred. I panicked. I didn't have a coach or a mentor, and I needed guidance. I remember grabbing my umbrella and walking to the neighborhood library looking for some comfort in a book on performance by an artist with experience—and perhaps some good advice for me. I asked the clerk if there were any books on stage performance for singer-songwriters. He was thin and tall, dressed in gray, matching our overcast day, wearing wire-rimmed glasses and a wee bit of an attitude.

"What kind of music is it?" he asked.

"Pop rock music. I'm in a band and we have our first show," I exclaimed.

"Rock music?" he responded with a dismissive shaking of the head. "Oh no, I think not." I was alone with my anxiety, with no one to help me, teach me, or ease my worry. And, I never found the book. I went on to perform for years, through the fear, and made oodles of mistakes along the way, all part of being in the world of entertainment. I had a vocal coach and feedback from friends, but still I wish I'd had a mentor. And to this day, I have found only one book about stage performance from a songwriter's point of view and seen very little about stage performance for musicians on film. After teaching songwriting and performance for the past ten years at Musicians Institute in Hollywood, California, helping hundreds of students find their way and develop their true artistry, I decided to write this book and film the DVD.

This is a personal undertaking in that I, too, suffered from severe stage fright, as many of us do. I don't believe it will ever completely go away, but I believe that one learns to work through it and that it lessens over time. I walked away from performing music at one point in my career to become a standup comedian. Talk about breaking down the wall. People would heckle me in the clubs, and I had to learn to win them over. Standup was like training in the boxing ring without gloves on. I guess I've always been more comfortable making people laugh than having them listen to me sing. How boring, how sad, how naked I felt. On the flip side, I am naturally playful, and learned an incredible amount about myself and the audience by doing standup. Soon, I began incorporating original comedy songs and imitating my favorite artists during my set. Ironically, I won an ASCAP songwriting award for a parody I wrote, called "I Want a Man with Muscles." We shot the music video with me wearing an eight-inch beehive hairdo, and 12 bodybuilders in bikinis dancing around me. It was a spoof making fun of glam metal rock bands, portraying supermodels as eye candy, set decoration, and for some strange reason straddling sports cars in every music video. Only this time, it was the men's turn to be exploited. Still, throughout it all, I somehow separated the songs of my heart from my cerebral comic material. Something remained missing.

When I went back into music full-time, I remained primarily a studio musician and began working with writing partner and producer Dean Landon. And when shopping our songs and demos, people wanted to know who was singing on them and, accidentally on purpose, I landed my first record deal. I then had to take the studio-recorded songs to the stage. I had to wear them like a coat, break them in, and make them mine. And even though I wrote them, understanding who I was as an artist and how I could best deliver these songs to an audience was challenging.

Over time, I learned that talking with the audience, making them laugh between numbers, and then sharing my heartfelt songs were all part of the same conversation. I finally brought my entire self onto the stage, instead of leaving her in the dressing room until after the show. I was present. Since then I've toured internationally, recorded three additional records, sang on national television and in concert stadiums, all part of a whole new and exciting world.

We write songs, but the art of performing them is an entirely different beast. Some artists are "naturals" at it, some should remain songwriters, and some can really flourish over time with a true understanding of what it is they are doing. Take away the piano we hide behind, take away the guitar we hug, move the mic stand we hold on to for dear life, and let the real conversation with the audience begin.

If you're reading this book, I wrote it to help you avoid spending as much time as I did, worrying and searching, and to grant you more time to bring beauty into the world with your music for audiences that await you.

MAKING
YOUR MARK
IN MUSIC

PART I

FROM THE INSIDE OUT

1

FINDING YOU

CAPTURING WHAT'S ALREADY THERE

"Music is love in search of a voice."
—LEO TOLSTOY

I n this chapter I am going to help you find the treasures you already hold. You've chosen a profession that is about performing. Maybe you didn't start with that in mind. It's a very strange thing to do, getting up onstage and saying, Hey, everyone—look at me! As a songwriter, my songs came from a less than "happy" place at first. They were more a reflection of my being an outcast in junior high, feeling angry and unheard in the world, and even getting heartbroken for the first time. I'd sit at the piano pouring my heart out and write a song about my plight. All artists' way of purging, one might say, is a form of therapy. So the very idea of taking that up onstage to share with the world—are you kidding me?

Truthfully, name one person who hasn't felt the emotions behind any of the subjects we write about: love, elation, anger, fear, loss, loneliness . . . And if you take a closer look, we perform in our everyday lives without even knowing it. Consider what's going on when you dress up for the day, ask for something you want, go out on a date, or walk into a party—you are performing. You have an intention, a mood, and a goal in mind that your interaction with other people will result in. When you participate in your everyday life, you are playing a part. You have an "on" switch and an "off" switch that you can fully access.

THE ON SWITCH. These are the times when you think, "I want to look good today," "I need him to say *yes*,"

"I want to fall in love," "I'm in the mood for a good time"—and your performance light turns on. We all know from experience what works for us: we know how to get what we want. When I'm feeling good, I put that energy out there, and end up having a good day. When I'm in a bad mood, I get caught in a traffic jam behind some slow car, and many obstacles build up throughout the day, because I'm enabling them.

THE OFF SWITCH. This occurs when we are inside our own thoughts and minds. We spend most of our time preoccupied with our to-do lists, in internal dialogue, and are often unaware of how we come across to others. Has anyone ever asked you if you are okay, when nothing was wrong? But for some reason, an expression on your face or something about your body language may have imparted the message that you were upset. And you most likely responded, "I'm fine"; you were probably just deep in thought and not thinking about how you came across to the world.

THE SWITCH YOU CANNOT USE. Your friends and family can read you like a book, because they know you. There are characteristics about you that are apparent to everyone else, though perhaps not to you.

So let's find out how much you know about yourself, and how you come across to others. Here are a few points of basic etiquette. All these things will apply to your everyday life as well as your stage persona and your journey through the music industry. Let's start at the very beginning.

MAKING AN IMPRESSION. Making an impression is an important opportunity you are given every day. How can you make a positive impact on others? We all know someone who has amazing charisma and seems to be liked by everyone. They light up a room when they enter. They make you feel good. What do they do to create this attractive energy? Here are some tips.

BODY LANGUAGE. A person generally knows in four seconds how they feel about you. Our body language speaks louder than words. And we all spend way too much time texting with our heads hanging down, looking at our cell phones, or slouched in a chair, shoulders forward and legs apart. I had a bad habit of standing with my arms folded or my hands on my hips.

But as I became more conscious of how people read my body language, I changed how I stood. I suggest you try standing up straight, shoulders back and walking with an intention of where you are heading. Take time to really look at your surroundings. Think outside your body. Appreciate the scenery and the people in it. Pretend that your eyes are a camera, and that you are filming your day and will play it back for someone less fortunate. Imagine a string at the top of your head lifting you up ever so gently toward the tip of the sky. Remember the feeling of a day, when you have your favorite outfit on, the sun is shining, you have an exciting event to go to, and you are feeling really good; your entire body language will change. People will respond to you differently.

EYE CONTACT. I live in Los Angeles and most people love to look at themselves. Have you ever had dinner with someone and there's a mirror behind you and they are checking themselves out the entire time? It's not fun. When in a room, make eye contact with the person to whom you're speaking. There's no bigger turnoff than someone who is talking to you and looking beyond you at the other people in the room. Or when someone keeps checking their cell phone, as if there's something more important than you. This tip should apply not only to people you are auditioning for, interviewing with, or asking for something from, but also to your friends, family, and sometimes even strangers. I also think it is important to smile with your eyes. Think positive thoughts about the person you are talking to, and there will be a little spark in your eye. The recipient will feel it and mirroring will come into play. Mirroring is when one person copies another in a social gathering. So this is a great way to bring out the best in others. If you send out positive energy, they will pick up on it and shine it back.

HANDSHAKE. Give a nice firm handshake when meeting someone. Have you ever had a wet-noodle handshake? Someone kind of shakes your hand and you end up holding on to part of his or her pinky finger. If you are a wet-noodler, you come across as though you're affected, think you're too good for anyone, or are a total germophobe! Imagine hugging someone without touching him or her, or blowing air kisses. Well, it's the same thing when it comes to a handshake. I can tell a lot about a person by the way they shake my hand. Don't get me wrong—the supersized squeezer shake until my hand is about to break is just as bad. Find a middle ground. A handshake tells a person how committed you are.

RESPECT. Something has been lost when it comes to showing respect for others. Quite often, you don't know the person to whom you are talking, and everyone has something that's worth learning. Even if you don't get what you want, people's time is valuable. Thank them for it. You might get the cold shoulder—it often happens. But try to be the bigger person and walk away politely and with dignity. This is a major lesson I have learned: never burn a bridge, the entertainment world is a small place, and you'll most likely meet that person again one day, work with them, or work with someone who knows them. So, if things don't work out, don't storm off, or pout, or slam the door, or hang up on them. No one owes you anything; on the other hand, if you do get something, consider it a gift.

FIND SOMETHING IN COMMON. When you are in conversation with someone, the best thing to do is find something you have in common. Are you from the same city? Do you like something they're wearing? There's always something to point out, and people love to talk about themselves. Let them shine, too.

So I've covered the basics on leaving a good impression wherever you go. And all of these tips help make others feel good, too. If you know someone who makes you feel good or special, you will want to be around them all the time. As performers we are conduits, telling stories to help the audience members understand themselves. It's not about "us"; it's about what we can share.

Finding You

The next section and questionnaire will begin exploring and revealing special characteristics that are inherent in you, and show you how to incorporate them in your musical persona.

STAGE NAME. A name has energy. It says a lot about you. When you choose a stage name, it should not be as common as Jim Smith (the most popular surname and baby name in the United States, according to an online statistics list). And it shouldn't be too difficult to pronounce or remember: "Ladies and Gentleman—please welcome to the stage Mishawkalya Tsu Hensvickty." (If any of you have that name, forgive me, I just made it up.) You can be creative and have fun when it comes to a name. My legal last name is Peress; everyone mispronounces it as "Perez," or "Press," or "Peeris." And with my first name, Anika (pronounced like "Monica" without the "M"), I've heard everything from "Happy Chanukah" to "An-eee-ka," to "Ann-eye-ka," to something even more ridiculous. When I was releasing my debut CD, I told the record label I wanted to use just "Anika." But lo and behold, there was already an Anika. I looked, and looked, and looked and finally just spelled my last name phonetically the way it is pronounced, "Paris." So if you're not crazy about your name, consider combining one exotic name with an easy one as I did: Anika Paris.

1. CREATE A UNIQUE STAGE NAME THAT DEFINES YOU. Try using your middle name, or dropping letters from your name. Or make one up, using your street name and your first pet's name, or a nickname people call you, or perhaps a cherished family name. Think about rhymes and meter and how the name rolls off the tongue. Try different syllables:

One syllable: Joan Jett
Two syllables: Ja-mie Cul-lum
Three syllables: Jen-ni-fer Ho-li-day

Alliterations are always good. This is where the first letter in both names is the same: for example, Lisa Lovelett, Christian Calloway.

Write down some stage names and try to create a new one. (You can always grab a baby name book at the bookstore, or look online for baby names or surnames to help you if you run out of ideas.)

_____

_____

_____

_____

_____

2. DESCRIBE YOUR OWN TYPE OF MUSIC. This is one of the hardest things to do. People will often ask you, What kind of music do you sing? Then we'll most likely sit around and take two artists and somehow become a hybrid of sorts. Many people answer the question by taking two artists and somehow becoming a hybrid of sorts. For example, I used to say I'm a cross between Sheryl Crowe and Norah Jones. And truthfully, I sound nothing like either of them, so it's a silly thing to try to do. Hybrids make for great cars—I love my Prius—but musical artists are not built to save on gas. In fact, we need as much gas as we can to keep going! I suggest creating your own style of music rather than comparing yourself to others. I call my music "confessional pop," and then let the listener decide to whom they want to compare me.

I've had students call their music acoustic soul, spoken jazz, rock revenge, sweet country, vintage soul, and more.

CREATE YOUR SOUND. What genre of music do you sing? Where do you think you fit in? Circle which one would apply to your songs and add your flavor.

POP	BLUES	ROCK	COUNTRY
SOUL	HIP HOP	GOSPEL	JAZZ
REGGAE	ELECTRONICA	SKA	CABARET
DANCE	MUSICAL THEATER	EMO	OTHER

_____

_____

_____

_____

_____

MATCH UP YOUR ANSWERS. Does the physical you match your stage name and musical style? You can't be a rocker who's lived her entire life in Bel Air, California, and drives a Mercedes and have the name Jennifer Star. Daddy's money doesn't buy you angst! If you aren't part of the country culture and you have the name Simone Fabergé, you can't be a country singer, as surely as I can't be a gangster rapper named Lady Lo Phat. I hope you're laughing right now. Some people will try—you'd be surprised. But remember, audiences will know when you lack authenticity. So be honest with yourself about your art and where it stems from and the identity you are creating. I always say, "No matter how hard you try, you can't run away from yourself."

3. DISCOVER YOUR PHYSICAL ASSETS. What do you think are your best assets? There is something wonderful in all of us. What is uniquely yours? Is it your eyes, your smile, your hair, your hand movements, your facial expressions, the way you walk?

_____

_____

_____

_____

_____

4. OWN YOUR OWN FASHION. Over the years, trends come and go. But we all have a style we feel most comfortable with. It could be a necklace we have and wear all the time, a watch, a certain pair of shoes, or perhaps a scarf. So ask yourself, what's that thing that you like wearing? (I know we all wear underwear, but that's not the answer!) I can't go without my:

_____

_____

_____

_____

_____

5. WORK WITH YOUR PERSONALITY. How would you describe yourself? Are you a party person, worker-driven, shy, serious, class clown, or other? (Even if you're shy or quiet, the mystery can be intriguing. I say if you want to capture someone's attention, whisper.)

_____

_____

_____

_____

_____

What do your friends say they thought about you on first impression versus now that they know you? (Here we can better understand how we are perceived by others, rather than how we think people see us.)

_____

_____

_____

_____

_____

How would your family describe you?

_____

_____

_____

_____

_____

6. FIND YOUR ESSENCE. Here's a cool game. Essences say a lot about your personality traits and how you come across to people. Your answers to these questions should not only be based on how you physically look and what you like. The answers should be about the feeling or essence of your characteristics and personality, so that if you were to describe the answers to a friend, he or she could guess that this person is you. For example, if you were describing someone's animal essence as that of a lion, you may say that this person demands attention, is in control, and can be both intimidating and beautiful. A dolphin is more of a cute person who is friendly, loyal, talkative, playful, and wants to please. Then you can switch to asking what color this person would be. A person whose essence is the color red most likely has a strong presence and is perhaps a bit loud, whereas someone whose essence is the color yellow would be more relaxed and cheerful, and so on. You're thus defining the overall spirit of the person, not just their physical attributes. I suggest playing this game with friends. Our perspectives and impressions of each other may shed some light on things we don't always know about ourselves.

If you were an animal, what animal would you be, and why?

_____

_____

_____

_____

_____

If you were a color, what color would you be, and why?

_____

_____

_____

_____

_____

If you were a season, what season would you be, and why?

_____

_____

_____

_____

_____

If you were a musical instrument, which one would you be, and why?

_____

_____

_____

_____

_____

If you were a book or movie, which one would you be, and why? (For example, a romantic comedy, a mystery, and so on.)

_____
_____
_____
_____
_____

You can go on as long as you like, discovering many different essences you can compare yourself to. Be creative: ask what kind of car, vacation, holiday, song, weather, painting, poem, body of water, kind of cereal.

_____
_____
_____
_____
_____

Summing up, I will continue to expand on many of the areas touched on in this chapter. And as you go through this book, little by little you'll peel back the layers and find what already lies beneath. It will help bring more of you to your songs, to your conversation, to your style, and to the impression you make.

Use this book as a journal; there are pages for you to write on, in order to discover more about yourself. Picasso once said, "To sing is to close your eyes and paint." So remember: just as writing a song takes time and thought and creativity, so will taking this journey toward self-discovery and learning how best to present and perform your music. It will be fun and thought provoking, and will require you to tap into your imagination.

How do some of the answers so far make you think differently? How do your answers create an overall feeling about yourself as an artist?

_____
_____
_____
_____
_____
_____
_____

2

BRIDGING THE GAP BETWEEN AUDIENCE AND THE STAGE

CASTING YOURSELF

"If music be the food of love, play on."
—William Shakespeare

It is showtime and you're waiting to go on. The nerves kick in, your heart is racing, the palms of your hands are sweating, and the adrenaline in your system is revving you up. Everybody fights this feeling, but you feel it because you care. In fact, I believe performers need it to get through a musical set, because performing requires extra energy. You ask yourself, will they like me? Will this evening and performance be a success? Success is simply when preparation meets opportunity. So the real question is, have you done your homework? Have you practiced to the point that you are truly confident you can perform your set with your eyes closed? Yes, we all know part of the excitement of performance is that it is in "real time" and there are no guarantees for perfection. The art of music is its free form, its ability to float in the room, provoke a mood, and alter a moment. Still, one must be prepared and resilient so that the spontaneity won't take you out of your performance flow.

You've chosen music as an extension of self-expression. It's like walking from the real world and bringing it onto the stage. Are you excited to share your story with the audience? How do you find your story? How do you bridge the gap between the audience and the stage? How do you cast yourself in this art form?

As I discussed in chapter 1, you must focus on what's already inherent within you. The beauty of music touches each and every one of us, when words alone fail. It is an invisible magic connecting our bodies, minds, and souls. Music is the only medium in which all races, creeds, and colors can gather side by side and sing in unison. As artists we live with a heightened awareness, perhaps feeling more deeply than many others, and gather information, stories, and memories and reflections of the world and share them through music and lyric. Now ask yourself what role you play in bringing this art and your message to your audience. There are different ways to present different genres of music. What is your genre and your style of presentation? How do you use music to express your opinions and point of view?

Here are five categories that I've created to help you identify your role within your musical experience. With each category I have listed artists spanning the past five decades. Reviewing these categories helps give you a clearer insight into the different musical genres and how each stage performance may differ. I recommend researching some of the artists I've mentioned if you have not already heard of them. Find out who your favorite artists studied, and familiarize yourself with artists from different generations. Learn what inspired them. In many ways musicians are passing on the baton to each new generation to continue sharing music with the world. We must honor their legacy and learn from the ones who came before. Take a look and see which category you identify with the most. How would you cast yourself?

CASTING YOURSELF	
1. SINGER SONGWRITER	THE FRIEND
2. POP ICON	THE PARTIER
3. CULTURAL MUSICIAN	THE EXAMINER
4. BAND MEMBER	THE COLLABORATOR
5. MUSICALLY GIFTED	THE MAGICIAN

1. THE SINGER-SONGWRITER (A.K.A. THE "FRIEND"). These artists collect events in life and share them with their audiences. Their shows are often like having your best friend in your living room, talking directly to you and sharing personal stories or world events in song. They often have a unique sound but don't need to have what I call "mad pipes." (They can sing more simply, with the honesty and purity of their voice being enough.) A few examples:

SINGER SONGWRITER	
1960	BOB DYLAN, WOODIE GUTHRIE, PETE SEEGER, JUDY COLLINS, NEIL DIAMOND
1970	CAROL KING, BILLY JOEL, NEIL YOUNG, CAT STEVENS, JAMES TAYLOR, JONI MITCHELL, ELTON JOHN
1980	BRENDA RUSSELL, AIMEE MAN, BRUCE SPRINGSTEEN, DAN FOLGELBERG, SHAWN COLVIN
1990	SARAH McLACHIN, SHERYL CROWE, ALANIS MORISSETTE, JEFF BUCKLEY
2000-2001 AND ON	JOHN MAYER, KT TUNSTALL, JASON MRAZ, GLEN HANSARD, AMOS LESS, COLBIE CAILLAT, SARAH BARIELLES

2. THE POP ICON (A.K.A. THE "PARTIER"). These artists have huge audiences and productions. Their shows escape from everyday life. Some create alter egos and some use shock tools such as stage theatrics, wild outfits, and sexuality to get the crowd's attention and turn the audience into group voyeurs. A few examples:

POP ICON	
1960	ELVIS PRESLEY
1970	OZZIE OSBOURNE, DAVID BOWIE, ALICE COOPER, MEATLOAF
1980	MICHAEL JACKSON, MADONNA, CHER, PRINCE
1990	MARILYN MANSON, SPICE GIRLS
2000-2010 AND ON	PINK, BRITNEY SPEARS, LADY GAGA, ADAM LAMBERT, KATIE PERRY

3. THE CULTURAL MUSICIAN (A.K.A. THE "EXAMINER"). These artists are defined by their culture. They are singers talking about the real world and life, in their hometowns, in the clubs, on the streets. They are a cultural phenomenon, reflecting and examining the era or times they live in. Usually hip-hop, country, and jazz music come under this category. (Note that there are also Latin, Caribbean, African, and many more genres of cultural music, but we are focusing on three main genres.) A few examples:

CULTURAL	
1950s - 60	**COUNTRY:** JOHHNY CASH, DOLLY PARTON, PATSY CLINE **JAZZ:** SINATRA, NAT KING COLE, TONY BENNETT, ELLA, BILLIE HOLIDAY
1970	**COUNTRY:** WILLIE NELSON, LORETTA LYNN, WAYLON JENNINGS **HIP HOP:** SUGAR HILL GANG **JAZZ:** HERBIE HANCOCK, CHICK COREA, DAVE BRUBECK
1980	**COUNTRY:** ANNE MURRAY, KENNY ROGERS, CRYSTAL GAYLE **HIP HOP:** GRANDMASTER FLASH, RUN DMC, LL COOL J **JAZZ:** HARRY CONNICK JR.
1990	**COUNTRY:** GARTH BROOKS, SHANIA TWAIN, LEANN RIMES **HIP HOP:** DR. DRE, MC HAMMER, NOTORIOUS, B.I.G., JAY Z., SNOOP DOG **JAZZ:** DIANA KRALL
2000-2011 AND ON	**COUNTRY:** DIXIE CHICKS, GRETCHEN WILSON, KENNY CHESNEY, TAYLOR SWIFT, CARRIE UNDERWOOD, LADY ANTEBELLUM, ZACK BROWN BAND **HIP HOP:** EMINEM, LIL JOHN, NELLY, MIA, KANYE WEST **JAZZ:** NORAH JONES, MICHAEL BUBLE, JAMIE CULLUM, ADELE

4. THE BAND MEMBER (A.K.A. THE "COLLABORATOR"). This is where you are part of an ensemble. Your fans and groupies are an extension—a collective conscience standing in unison. Each member is a piece of the pie, creating a colorful palette and a cult following. A few examples:

BANDS	
1960	BEATLES, BYRDS, ROLLING STONES, THE BEACH BOYS, LOVIN SPOONFUL
1970	ABBA, HEART, QUEEN, EAGLES, THE DOORS, LED ZEPPELIN, PINK FLOYD, STEVE MILLER BAND, JACKSON FIVE, THE YARD BIRDS, AREOSMITH, THE SUPREMES, EMMERSON LAKE AND PALMER, REO SPEEDWAGON, EARTH WIND AND FIRE, STEPPENWOLF, FLEETWOOD MAC, YES
1980	VAN HALEN, BON JOVI, GENESIS, DURAN DURAN, BLACK SABATH, STYX, DEF LEPPARD, CHICAGO, AMERICA, SEALS AND CROFT, BANGLES, THE GO-GOS, HALL AND OATES, U2
1990	NIRVANA, GUNS N ROSES, PEARL JAM, RED HOT CHILI PEPPERS, SMASHING PUMPKINS, CREED, ALICE IN CHAINS
2000-2011 AND ON	DAVE MATHEWS BAND, MAROON 5, LINKIN PARK, MUSE, COLDPLAY, INCUBUS, EVANESCENCE, WHITE STRIPES, TRAIN, NO DOUBT, RADIOHEAD, DIXIE CHICKS, FOO FIGHTERS, BLACK EYED PEAS, GREEN DAY, WILCO, PARAMORE

5. THE MUSICALLY GIFTED (A.K.A. THE "MAGICIAN"). These artists are well known for their outstanding musical gift. They don't need much more than a stage and the chance to show off their voice and/or instrumental magic. A few examples *(see following page)*:

MAGICIANS	
1960	MARVIN GAYE, SMOKEY ROBINSON, GLADYS KNIGHT, JAMES BROWN, BARBRA STREISAND
1970	ARETHA FRANKLIN, JANIS JOPLIN, JIMI HENDRIX, JOE COCKER, TINA TURNER, PATTI LA BELLE, FREDDIE MERCURY, BB KING, ERIC CLAPTON, STEVIE WONDER, DONNY HATHAWAY
1980	WHITNEY HOUSTON, MARIAH CAREY, STING, STEVE PERRY, MICHAEL BOLTON, CYNDI LAUPER
1990	MELISSA ETHERIDGE, CARLOS SANTANA, CELINE DION
2000-2010 AND ON	CHRISTINA AGUILLERA, BEYONCE, KELLY CLARKSON, ANDRE BOCELLI, JOSS STONE

Choose which category you feel fits closest to you and your style of music, and consider its "authenticity factor." Make sure that the way you cast yourself is consistent with your voice, your physical look, your age, and your personality. You may relate to more than one category, but choose which rings most true for you. You are the instrument connecting your message with the audience. How do people relate to you in life, and how will you relate to your audience in song? Circle one below.

Singer-Songwriter

Pop Icon

Cultural Musician

Band

Musically Gifted

Once you've cast yourself, explore ways in which to make your performance a natural extension of you. How do you do that? By getting to the core of what your role as an entertainer means.

1. Are you going to intimately share with your audience a story they can relate to?
2. Are you going to let them forget reality for a moment by entering a fantasy world that you create?
3. Are you going to sing about how to change the way things are in the world today?
4. Are you going to mesmerize them with your extraordinary ability?

Because whatever you decide to do, remember that music is a lot more powerful than solely performing in a show. Here's an excerpt from one of my favorite speeches that I have my students read aloud the first day of class. In his welcoming address in September 2004, Karl Paulnack, the head of the music department at Boston Conservatory, told the following to the freshman class:

> If we were a medical school, and you were here as a med student practicing appendectomies, you'd take your work very seriously because you would imagine that some night at 2 a.m., someone is going to waltz into your emergency room and you're going to have to save their life. Well, my friends, someday at 8 p.m. someone is going to walk into your concert hall and bring you a mind that is confused, a heart that is overwhelmed, a soul that is weary. Whether they go out whole again will depend partly on how well you do your craft. You're a lot closer to a paramedic, a firefighter, a rescue worker. You're here to become a sort of therapist for the human soul, a spiritual version of a chiropractor, physical therapist, someone who works with our insides to see if they get things to line up, to see if we can come into harmony with ourselves and be healthy and happy and well. Frankly, ladies and gentlemen, I expect you not only to master music; I expect you to save the planet. If there is a future wave of wellness on this planet, of harmony, of peace, of an end to war, of mutual understanding, of equality, of fairness, I don't expect it will come from a government, a military force, or a corporation. I no longer even expect it to come from the religions of the world, which together seem to have brought us as much war as they have peace. If there is a future of peace for humankind, if there is to be an understanding of how these invisible, internal things should fit together, I expect it will come from the artists, because that's what we do.

In other words, you play an important role as an entertainer, and so fully understanding who you are is essential. I too believe that psychology and music are closely related and that music has the ability to move the invisible pieces inside us. After teaching for many years, I went to graduate school and completed some master classes in psychology. I briefly considered becoming a counselor, since coaching performance and songwriting addresses a lot of personal issues with students. I learned a lot about the human psyche and found it fascinating. Some personality tests have been developed to help guide people in careers, in life, and in love. I feel they can be applied to artists as they are developing their careers. One test in particular is called the Myers-Briggs Type Indicator (or MBTI, also known as Jung Typology), designed to measure your psychological preferences and the basic dimensions of human behavior. It examines the way people communicate and act, our words and our deeds, or, simply what we say and what we do. These preferences were created by Carl Gustav Jung and published as his collective works in his book *Psychological Types*. The questions are designed to define how you perceive the world and make everyday decisions. Learning more about your inherent qualities will help your performance. So later I'm going to ask you to take the test and use the results for creative development. I've taken the MBTI at different times in my life, and it is informative and fun!

Martha Velez and Bob Marley.

Before you take the test, I want to give some feedback and insight from a professional in the field. Martha Velez is an amazing renaissance woman. She is a therapist who holds an MA degree from Antioch University and a PhD from Pacifica Graduate Institute in cultural mythology and depth psychology, and she is an incredibly talented singer and actress. Martha's booming singing career started when she won an opera scholarship as a mezzo-soprano at the age of twelve, which eventually led to a successful music and recording career. Her debut album, *Fiends and Angels*, was released on Sire Records and features such greats as Eric Clapton, pianist Christine McVie (Fleetwood Mac), and drummer Mitch Mitchell (Jimi Hendrix), among many other great British musicians. She traveled to Jamaica to compose and record with reggae star Bob Marley and his group the Wailers, which included guitarist Al Anderson. Martha is the only artist for whom Marley functioned as record producer. As an actor in television and film, Martha has worked alongside Samuel L. Jackson, Julianne Moore, Halle Berry, the late Patrick Swayze, and Dennis Hopper, to name a few. Martha Velez has many stories to tell in her forthcoming book, *Singing with the Great Music Monsters*. Few artists could better understand the relationship between music, psychology, and performance than Martha. Here is some of Martha's wisdom.

Q: What interested you in becoming a therapist after having such a successful career in music and acting?

A: Psychological subtext and subliminal emotional underpinnings are the direct ingredients for creating a role or writing and singing a song. As a performer, I was always interested in that component—the emotional energy it takes to flesh out a role and the soulful energy that is demanded when creating a piece of music. In my musical journey, I went from folk music to blues-rock, reggae, and finally singer-songwriter music. At each turn, [having] a particular awareness was critical: What was the truth in what I was singing, and how could I best convey the soul of that to the audience so that they too could share in the experience? As your wonderful quote by Karl Paulnack expresses: You're a sort of therapist for the human soul—the artist does become a critical ingredient in the emotional interfacing with the individual in the audience. The musician is a therapist in the unconscious search for self and for the soul/psyche of the audience. The convergence of the two, musician/entertainer and audience, is a psychological bond: when positive it is healing; when negative it can be disturbing. As artists, our effort is to be healing. As a therapist, it is the same effort. As the singing therapist, I get to have both worlds. But, your question was why I moved from music to therapy. It was to have a tool by which I could truly understand the psychological interaction that I had been experiencing with audiences for so many years. It was a fascinating subject for me through which I could analyze deeper layers of psyche that emerge naturally when an artist is invested in the truth of their work. It is bond a therapist creates with a patient when creating the container of trust leading to the journey of healing.

Q: If there were something you could have known within yourself earlier in your life as an entertainer, what would it be? Has that self-awareness changed your performance in any way today?

A: It would have been to trust myself more. Although I had training and moved into a professional world relatively early, I was always riddled with self-doubt. When I worked with the truth of the work, the doubt evaporated. The consciousness of that reality led to an unconscious trust in the work, which allowed for a psychological, emotional, and physical release in my body, ultimately allowing me to diffuse the doubt through "living in the trust" of the work. Today, I would say that my self-awareness is manifested through greater relaxation through meditation, a kind of deliverance to the music, creating a zone that releases tensions, and concentration that allows me to live in the sound—essentially, to trust. This may come from years of doing, but also from allowing for the beauty of certain imperfections. Perfection can kill the beauty of natural soul vibrations.

Q: Many artists are younger during the peak of their performing days. How important do you feel it is to understand yourself and your role as an entertainer?

A: Above all an artist, especially a younger one, needs a vital support system. With those surrounding them who encourage a healthy physical and psychological balance. In the '60s there were many incredible artists who lived in their music and the rock 'n' roll life without any self-awareness or professional analysis. They turned to artificial forms of relaxation, which ruined their bodies and ultimately, in some cases, their abilities and lives. Great musicians, such as Eric Clapton, were almost ruined by drugs as a false fix for relaxation. Gratefully, Eric rehabilitated himself and continued in a flourishing career. Today, there is a greater awareness about the sanctity of the artist as a human being performing within the parameters of growth and development. That is, of course, if there is a positive support system surrounding the artist. As a wise sage said, "Stay close to those people who truly love you and run from the people who don't." The fact is that artists work within an entertainment industry whose bottom line is not always the sanctity of the human being as an artist, but rather the dollar. I've always said, the music industry eats its young. Having said that, the industry is also an exciting, exhilarating place for an artist to realize the full potential of creating a viable career, reaching their larger audience potential and creating a nest egg for the future of their lives and their progeny. Critical to the longevity of an artist is the understanding of your individuality, how you define your role as an artist. What are the goals that you set, how do you really map that out, how willing are you to digress from that path, and what kind of time frame makes sense? Most artists will be doing some form of their art forever. The art itself is a therapy for the artist. When that therapy, as art, reaches the audience, it is a kiss from the universe.

Q: Can you talk a bit about stage fright? Did you ever have it? Why might one feel fearful in one area and not another?
A: As mentioned earlier, I had self-doubt, which I ameliorated. I never really had the classic stage fright that some artists speak of. Stage fright in my opinion is a form of a panic attack, a hypervigilance about perfection, a fear of failure, and in some cases, a fear of success. As an actor, I was trained at the High School of Performing Arts, then studied at Strasberg, and [then] in a master class with Uta Hagen. In each training program, relaxation exercises were taught. One was to jump up and down, which I still do when I am performing in theater. As a singer, I always vocalized before performing and practiced breathing. It is amazing how we forget to breathe when we are anxious about our performance. Anxiety is a key source for stress, and the actual act of performing is generally a form of release. If you can do exercises before beginning to perform, as if you were in the actual act of performing, then you can get on to the stage, not just warmed up, but psychologically partway into the zone of performance. There will be no room for stage fright. As everyone knows, preparation is the key to flying. We can't fly in all areas of our lives, but we can when we fulfill the joy of our art. So, fly from fright. Fright can be analyzed and diffused. Fly with your art! While in the wings, visualize yourself onstage, having already given a brilliant performance. Fly!

Q: What are your thoughts about using the Myers-Briggs Type Indicator Questionnaire or any other psychological aptitude tests as tools for an artist's self-discovery?
A: The MBTI is an interesting test. It promotes a very quick assessment

of an individual's leanings toward a potential behavioral pattern that may or may not manifest completely, but most likely does manifest in a certain percentage of behavioral areas. I think it is helpful as a mild barometer of behavior, but definitely not as the bible of behavior modification. An individual who is struggling with some basic adjustment issues can use this test as a monitor for their basic incremental growth. An individual who is dealing with troubling issues would need a more rigorous test to diagnose those problems that are deeply embedded in their body memory and, consequently, may be causing behavior patterns that may lead to difficulties coping, and may even be at the root of something like stage fright. When a condition like stage fright is crippling an artist, then individual psychotherapy is recommended. However, I think the MBTI is a fine tool for cursory exploration of general attitude and behavior on a first-layer level.

Q: Do you feel that music is instrumental in healing the human psyche?

A: As has been said, music soothes the savage beast. I might add that it fires the soul, it quiets the baby, it causes love to ignite. Music is a direct vibration to the human experience. It directly can recall a beautiful moment in life, as well as a mournful one. The artist's responsibility, as a healer through music, is to elevate life. Basic insecurities are inherent in so many areas of daily life, in so many career paths. Music has the ability to transfer energy. Music as an art form is classic transference—that is, when a therapist and patient resonate to the same emotional experience. A musician's job is to create transference. The musician moves their music through the vibration of their physical being to that of another human being. It is a moment of truth.

Q: Anything else you'd like to share?

A: I find this whole exploration of music, psyche, and healing very inspiring.

Thank you Martha for your thoughtful insight.

So let's continue on our quest! There is a free Meyers-Briggs/Jung Typology test that you can participate in online. Take a moment and find out what personality type you are by answering the questions provided. I'm going to do something rather nonconventional and more creative with your results and see how they can be applied to enhance your artistic vision.

First go to the Human Metrics website at www.humanmetrics.com. Click on the Jung Typology test in the upper left-hand corner of the page to take the test. Once you've completed the test, read about your results in the links provided. You can also follow along as I take you step by step in Appendix A.

Now take a look at the following Type Results Chart below, and find your match. Even if your results are not Composer or Performer (neither were mine!), don't panic. Everyone reading this book is pursuing a career in music and performance—so let's say it is a given. You can still get good insight into your innate qualities. With the additional results, you are going to create fun tools to enlighten and inspire you.

Type Results

GUARDIAN 40-45% Serve & Preserve	ARTISAN 30-35% The Artist	IDEALIST 15-20% Helping Others	RATIONALIST 5-10% The Problem Solvers
ISTJ Inspector	ISFJ Protector	INFJ Counselor	INTJ Mastermind
ISTP Crafter	ISFP Composer	INFP Healer	INTP Architect
ESTP Promoter	ESFP Performer	ENFP Champion	ENTP Inventor
ESTJ Supervisor	ESFJ Provider	ENFJ Teacher	ENTJ Field Marshall

Taking this test is very interesting, and you may relate to other famous people in your category. We are all extroverts, introverts, thinkers, feelers, judgers, perceivers, and intuitive at different times in our lives. Whether your result is Inspector, Protector, Counselor, Mastermind, Crafter, Composer, Healer, Architect, Promoter, Performer, Champion, Inventor, Supervisor, Provider, Teacher, or Field Marshall—all of these types can become part of your creative process.

Here, I am adding some crafty thinking on your part. You may be wondering, how does my personality type result help me as a musician? It measures what would be natural for you to pursue. So let's take the result, expand upon it, and apply it to music. Use your creativity and think outside of the box, with the right side of your brain—the random, intuitive, and subjective side of the brain. And, use your type to inspire you by looking up your type-result descriptive word on thesaurus.com.

How would this work if your type were Architect ENTP, as an example.

You can use the meaning and synonyms of the word "architect" to draw ideas from. Apply the synonyms you like to developing your persona, your song choices, your visual ideas and themes, and whatever they ignite in you. Use them as creative platforms and build from there.

I'll take you through the steps.

SEARCHING FOR SYNONYMS. First, what does "architect" mean? An architect starts with a plan, pours the foundation, then builds and creates beautiful visuals and spaces. An architect also designs and leaves permanent landmarks. Here are synonyms for the word "architect" that I found on thesaurus.com: *author, brain, creator, deity, designer, founder, generator, initiator, maker, originator, producer, sire.* An architect can be a designer of many things, not just buildings. They can be a world architect, a body architect, even a life architect—you choose. One of my favorite architects is Frank Gehry, who breaks all the conventional rules by allegedly crumpling up pieces of paper to begin his process of design, using the odd shapes as models. He expands on that convention by using his intuition and precision to complete the projects. His buildings often look like spaceships and are spectacular monuments that will last centuries. When he designed the concert hall in downtown Los Angeles, he spoke about creating a space that would acoustically enrich the sound for the orchestra, and he designed the seating to allow a close visual interaction between the audience and the stage, thus creating a stronger connection. He is a true artist, who believes the musical experience must be "had by all." And if you've seen his buildings they literally bend, as shown below.

Collecting Images and Creating a Collage

Here are some images I've collected relating to architecture that caught my eye. I'll have you look up images with your result type in the worksheet at the end of this chapter, where you are allowed to give yourself permission to get in the sandbox and have fun!

Examples of How To Apply It

Okay, now let's see how you can continue even further by pairing the word "architect" with each of the five categories of performer types you were asked to cast yourself in earlier. How would an Architect type result apply in this case?

1. IF YOU ARE A SINGER-SONGWRITER. Perhaps you could design a set list of songs using the idea of looking through the windows of an apartment building, and create stories going on inside each room.

2. IF YOU ARE A POP ICON. You can make the layout of your stage various levels. For example, have someone sitting, someone standing on a block, and someone off the raised stage to create the impression that the viewer is looking in a building with different floors. You could have dancers posing in the shape of a pyramid, and visuals of highs and lows all connecting to create a great image.

3. IF YOU ARE A CULTURAL MUSICIAN (COUNTRY, JAZZ, OR RAP.) Why not write, sing, scat, or rap about the blueprints of the town or city you live in? How have the streets you grew up on changed? How has the culture changed? What lies beneath it all? Sing about the history and all the untold stories that happened there.

4. IF YOU ARE A BAND MEMBER. Create a unique costume idea. Maybe each member of the band can be part of a visual whole: for example, each player's shirt could have a piece of a visual that has been cut into puzzled pieces—and when you all stand side by side, the complete design can be seen.

5. IF YOU ARE A MAGICIAN. You may not know this, but architects often use a system called CAD on computers. It is a three-dimensional program used for designing structures. It is very advanced and pretty awesome. Perhaps integrate high-tech gadgets and computerized images to create a futuristic show.

See how it can open your mind to think more broadly, and how much fun you can have and how inventive you can be by applying personality results? Take your result now, and try doing some of what I just showed you.

My Type Result

Synonyms for this are:

_____

_____

_____

_____

_____

_____

_____

Collect images from various places, magazines, the Internet, your own collection, and paste them below. Create a collage, something to give you a visual palette to work with.

_____

_____

_____

_____

_____

_____

_____

How does my type result relate to my cast type—whether Singer-Songwriter, Pop Icon, Cultural Musician, Band, or Musically Gifted?

_____

_____

_____

_____

_____

_____

Let's add a little bit of spice! In addition to your Meyers-Briggs test result, your type falls under one of the Four Temperaments. It's located on the top row of the Type Results Graph on page 25 and in full detail at www.keirsey.com and the links provided for you in Appendix A on page 137. Are you the Guardian, the Idealist, the Artisan, or the Rationalist?

What celebrities in the arts are the same as you? Now let's play a bit more.

Putting It All Together

1. Choose your musical genre from the five categories listed at the beginning of the chapter.
2. Take your Meyers-Briggs test result, find synonyms, and create collages.
3. Now discover which of the Four Temperaments you fall under.
4. Find what other celebrities are the same as you.

Below is an example of how to put it all together. (You will do the same with your result type at the end of this chapter.)

> I am a singer-songwriter.
> My Myers-Briggs type is an Architect.
> I am a Rationalist.

Some celebrities that fall under the Rationalist Group are the following:

- Walt Disney, a film producer and a popular showman, as well as an innovator in animation and theme parks, was famous for building a dream world for children.
- Mark Twain, the author best known for writing *The Adventures of Tom Sawyer and Huckleberry Finn*: famous novels about the Midwest and adventures of a young man's quest for freedom and equality.
- George Bernard Shaw, the author of *Pygmalion*, a rags-to-riches story of a young woman and her metamorphosis from a commoner into a sophisticated lady.

All these celebrities who are Architects are fictional writers and visionaries. Perhaps their themes, stories, and characters could be incorporated into your show, your songs, and your delivery as an artist, and your songs. Let's revisit the idea of an apartment building (an evening of songs), with each room and floor holding different stories. On the first floor are stories or songs about yearning for freedom, the middle floor has songs about metamorphosis and change, and the top floor has songs about finding your dream. You talk about this place where all these people live. Make it a theme for the night or use it for a concept album and call it *High Rise*. Where is this building? Who are these people in each room? What are their stories?

Take all the different visuals and images you will be collecting, all the word associations you'll discover, all the stories of others in your category, and use them to add to your vision.

You now know a little more about how you interact in life and how others perceive you, as well as other famous artists who share your same personality results. Doing these exercises allows you to start creating some new ideas in nonconventional ways to open up your creativity. It's your vision, your songs, and your style of communicating that you're seeking.

I'll talk more in chapters to come about the actual physical things that one can do onstage to connect with their audience. So far, I've been designing the playground these past two chapters. Allow yourself to journal on the next few questions and let your artistic visions come to light!

Personality Questionairre

I am a (circle one):

      Singer-Songwriter

      Pop Icon

      Cultural Musician

      Band

      Musically Gifted

My Myers-Briggs personality type is:

_____

My descriptive noun is _____ , and the synonyms I found that I can use are:

_____
_____
_____
_____
_____

I am a (circle one):

      Guardian

      Idealist

      Artisan

      Rationalist

What part of my temperament relates to me the most?

_____
_____
_____
_____
_____

How can I apply these findings to a new vision in my music? (Perhaps a passion or platform?)

_____

_____

_____

_____

_____

_____

_____

What's a similarity shared by all the celebrities in my category? How do I relate to them? How do I differ from them?

_____

_____

_____

_____

_____

_____

What new ways can I communicate with the audience through my songs? Did any discoveries give me ideas for new subjects?

_____

_____

_____

_____

_____

_____

_____

How can I add a visual aid to design my show?

_____

_____

_____

_____

_____

_____

Other ideas. (Here's a chance to brainstorm, collect pictures, quotes, and stories, colors, and anything that inspires you. Create a mood board. Don't edit yourself if it leads you off the beaten path. Instead, go with it.)

_____

_____

_____

_____

_____

_____

_____

_____

_____

_____

_____

_____

_____

_____

_____

_____

_____

3

THREE POINTS OF VIEW

YOUR LYRIC IS YOUR CONVERSATION

"Music is the poetry of the air."
—JOHANN PAUL RICHTER

Y ou've cracked the oyster open and are shining up the pearl, discovering new things about yourself and your musical genre, applying personality tests and creative exercises to help you discover new ways to present yourself. Perhaps some new songs and material will soon be on the way. But in this chapter, I will discuss specific techniques showing you how to let your lyrics be your conversation and communication with your audience.

You learn the alphabet, how to talk, and how to walk from your parents; you learn how to drive instructed by a state official; and you go to school and learn from teachers. If you are going into the world of business, you've got a boss, a mentor, taking you through the steps needed to achieve your goals. But you stand onstage to sing and have no idea how or what you're supposed to do. Why? Because no one can tell you how to be yourself. Performing music is the only entertainment medium in which you play you. What method teaches that? Actors get taught how to envelop a character, become another person while the audience watches invisibly. But there is no fourth wall in music. Your performance is a musical version of your life, and the way you see it—and then, you're having to share that with the audience directly. Where's the "how to" book on that? Finally, here is a book that can lead you through those fearful steps.

Talk to any doctor: thank goodness there is medical school and other doctors teaching them how to do their job. Can you imagine if you were told, "Just go in there and operate!" Well, the end result for us as musical performers is not life and death, but what are we supposed to do? Just get up onstage and perform blindly and after a while figure it out? Yeah, good luck! Besides thrashing your head about as a rocker, or crying behind your guitar or the piano as a singer-songwriter—all the clichéd things you think you ought to do—there is so much more to delivering a song than you've been told. Your lyric is your conversation. I guess one could call it a simpler version of acting for singers. How to communicate what it is you're trying to say onstage is done in much the same way off stage. And one of the reasons I have had you take these personality tests along the way is to help you discover who you are in everyday life and how others may perceive you in order to help you be open to your style of communication and get creative doing so.

I remember now why I became a songwriter. It's not because I was popular and the head cheerleader, or one who could easily express herself through the awkward years of adolescence. Far from it. I couldn't say what I was thinking at the actual time. I am still a delayed-reaction person. Perhaps it takes time to process things. Every time a dire situation would come up or I was asked how I felt, I would freeze or answer like a people pleaser, with "Okay!" I would leave having said nothing, the wrong thing, or blabbering like an idiot. Later I would play things over and over again in my head, thinking "What is wrong with me?" Oh, if I had only said, (insert genius quote here), it would have been perfect. I'm sure you've been there. It happens to us all. But I found my voice in songs. The beautiful thing is that songs allow us to do that. All art forms allow us to create that scene again, capture it forever, or re-create a perfect scenario in which everything falls into place, the music is swelling, the words depict all that you are feeling inside, you are painting the perfect picture, you know the listener is hearing you, and BAM! You can rest now. And hopefully listeners will use your song as a means to heal themselves, or as a point of revenge. Who knows!

Let's talk about the three different points of view we use when we converse.

- We talk to ourselves (sometimes, surprisingly, out loud).
- We confide in one friend, family member, or lover.
- We tell a group of people what's going on.

You should apply the same viewpoints to your lyrics. Read your lyrics aloud as you would a monologue. How would you say the lines to somebody if they were sitting in front of you? Forget about singing them—just say them out loud. Hear what you are feeling. On every line, mark whether you are talking to yourself, to one person, or to a roomful of people. Sometimes it's a combination of more than one. But it is extremely helpful and pulls you back into the story, which is the raw reason you chose to sing this song, or the raw reason you decided to write the song. Your autopilot must be put to rest at this point; you don't want to just go through the motions—you want you to feel it again. And you must revisit the raw emotions of what you are trying to say, as well as how you want your audience to react.

TALKING TO YOURSELF. What does one do when talking to oneself? Often people look down or off to the side. Have you ever been midconversation with a friend and your internal dialogue comes out? You blurt out, "You know what? I left my wallet at home!" This is said out loud, really to alert yourself, but you are still in a conversation. Or perhaps you're cleaning up your room and suddenly you say, "Here it is! I've been looking all over for this," as if someone is there to share the experience with you. There are lines like these in songs. For example, one might sing, "No matter what, I'll be okay." You're reassuring yourself. Think about the last time you saw a movie in which the actor is silent and thinking. The audience is in sync with the actor's thinking process while it is happening. And it's as though you can hear the voice in the actor's head; sometimes there's even a narration or voice-over. It is the same idea with a song, but sung to yourself.

TALKING TO ONE PERSON. This should be easy enough. It is the basis of communication. But perhaps it can be fulfilled only if you have your cell phone and your texting alert sound muted for an extended period of time. Hard to do in today's information-hemorrhaging climate that would rank up there with *Guinness Book of World Records* these days. So let's defy the odds. Consider, when you have real quality time one-on-one, how you would express your thoughts to one individual. In a song you must be able to see their face and feel what it is you are trying to say to them. Tell them, "No matter what, I'll be okay."

TALKING TO A ROOMFUL OF PEOPLE. This has become my everyday job because I am an instructor. I talk to a roomful of people everyday. There are some people who need to do this in their everyday lives. They are probably very lonely and therefore talk to everyone; whether they're in line at the bank, or in a movie theater, or at the grocery store, they tweet on Twitter, post on Facebook, and announce to the world all their thoughts and emotions. When you're onstage however, you are given permission to do so. And we, the audience in this case, want to know what's going on. So addressing an entire room when communicating a lyric is much like sharing with everyone. Do you know what I mean? Have you ever felt this way? Have you ever had this happen to you? It's a way of letting people know they are in on the story. Tell them all, "No matter what, I'll be okay."

Now try it. Stand in front of a mirror and see what it looks like when saying, "No matter what, I'll be okay" from three points of view. Take your time, make sure to breathe, and feel how different each point of view feels.

How would you say it to yourself under your breath? What happens to your body language?

How would you tell someone else? Practice this by saying it to a friend. Or take a photograph and tell the person in the picture. Feel the connection with your eyes.

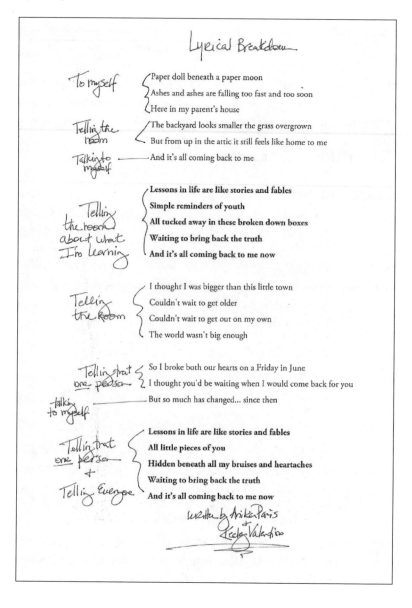

How would you announce it to a roomful of people? Imagine yelling it out the window to all your neighbors, or telling people on the streets as you're passing them by, or telling everyone online at Starbucks, or at a party. How would it feel?

Let's use some of my lyrics from a song called "Paper Dolls" as an example of how to break down a lyric into three points of view, so then you can apply these same lyric breakdowns to your songs.

Make notes about the lyrics you want to sing, and think about the subtext of the story. Read it aloud again with each assigned point of view. Try closing your eyes; try looking at a photograph of someone until their image is easily seen in your mind and you can pretend they are standing in the back row of the room. Pretend you had to tell everyone about an event going on by using the chorus lyrics of your song. And even if you've sung the song one hundred times, really listen to what you're saying. Sing it as though you know that someone in the room is going through the exact same thing. I also highly recommend you videotape yourself and play it back to see what it looks like. If you don't have access to a camera, use your laptop or your cell phone. Lastly, if you can't do this with any of these devices, simply rehearse in the mirror.

I suggest you practice singing to *three* spots in your rehearsal room. And let's talk about where to look when trying to impart these points of view.

SINGING TO YOURSELF. When singing to yourself, either look slightly down or close your eyes. Think inwardly when singing to yourself.

SINGING TO ONE PERSON. This helps create a focal point. Tape a photograph on the back wall of your rehearsal room. Sing to the photograph as though it's the character in the song. Keep referring back to that same picture, that same spot and sing directly to that character each time. (I often use a photograph on my music stand in the recording studio as well, so that I have someone to connect with emotionally by seeing his or her face.)

SINGING TO THE ROOM. Performing for a roomful of people requires more energy. Your body language opens up, and you want to make sure that everyone, including the back of the room, can hear you. Stand in the middle of the stage, spread your arms, and project your voice to the entire room.

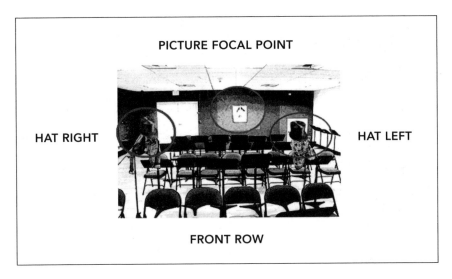

Let's create a good practice area for you and a fake audience. Place a hat on a mic stand, or grab some folding chairs—anything to give you points of view. (Pillows are good for visual points of reference.) Place something a few feet directly in front of you to represent the first row. Then, halfway between you and the back walls, place objects to the left and the right; this represents the center row. Again, tape a photograph of someone on the back wall for a focal point. Use all these various points to represent the audience. When practicing try performing for the front row, sing to the audience to your right and to your left, and perform for the back of the room. Tell everyone what's going on in the story of the song. If you are shy about direct eye contact at your next live performance, a trick is to look above the eyes at people's forehead or their hairline; they'll never know the difference. Practice all three points of view once you have your fake audience.

This chapter has visual examples in the DVD that comes with this book. Please refer to it for more insights. Above is an example of my own rehearsal room with a fake audience!

4

USING YOUR CHAKRAS

PAIRING THE PHYSICAL AND THE EMOTIONAL

"That's what music is: entertainment. The more you put yourself into it, the more of you comes out in it."
—Kurt Cobain

Now that you've gone through the steps of how to break down a lyric and practice emotionally connecting with each point of view, you might still be asking what to do with your body? This next chapter will explore how to pair the emotional self with the physical self.

In today's visually driven media world, the average attention span is about seven seconds. So you must keep your audience's interest and show them how you are feeling. There are many things about the body that tell us how someone feels. There are energy points and invisible connections because our bodies have a language of their own. When you are feeling nervous, for example, you often fold your arms and retract, much like a turtle crawling back into its shell. When you are angry and upset, you yell, thrust your body forward as if you're about to pounce like a lion, a tiger, or a cat. When you are happy and laughing out loud, you wiggle, jiggle, and completely let go for a moment. When you are sad you wilt, hold your stomach, sometimes even buckle at the knees unable to sustain your own body weight. So many things that happen are involuntary. Dancers have trained for years and hold a keen ability to express such beauty and emotion through movement. But many singers and performers forget all about the body and rely solely on their voice. Body movement is one of the most important elements, since your voice is directly connected to your body. I hear the following statement from students all the time: I don't know what to do with my hands. How do I stand? Where do I look? And they proceed to sing a song with their hands glued to their sides or gripping onto the mic stand or looking down and closing their eyes the entire song. Truth be told, if your body isn't open, your voice will suffer.

I took a wonderful class called the Vocal Body Movement Workshop in college. Every time I moved my body, I had to give it a sound. If I touched my toes, I had to mimic with my voice what bending over would sound like. In this movement, my voice would descend as I leaned toward the floor. I could not do it in silence. If I rolled on the floor, I had to make a sound "describing" what turning over felt like each time I turned, letting my voice roll, too. If I lifted my arm, my voice would ascend up the scale; when I lowered it back down, a descending tone with the movement would follow. Clapping my hands would be mimicked with a staccato sound, and on and on. It was a little strange at first, but we all wore workout clothes, had mats on the floor, and did many different types of exercises to open the voice and free the body, mind, and soul. I often use this exercise with vocal students as a warm-up. I suggest you take some sort of movement class to pair your voice and your body. I love yoga. It's nonimpact exercise to keep one balanced, focused, and relaxed. I suggest doing some sort of dance, or Pilates, or—my favorite—Cardioke (created and taught by Billy Blanks Jr. and Sharon Blanks, and if you don't live in Los Angeles, it's available in Target stores and online), a class in which one sings while doing aerobics. It helps build up stamina, self-confidence, and vocal power. And it is so much fun!

Now, let's look into the energy that our bodies hold. In Hinduism, energy centers have names and colors, creating a philosophy of *chakras*—wheel, or turning, energy centers along the spine. There are many ways to connect those energy centers and use the body to impart emotions through music and song.

Marcel Marceau, the great French mime, worked with my grandmother Anita Velez-Mitchell, a professional dancer and Broadway performer, and the late, great Michael Jackson, among countless others. In fact the famous moonwalk came about as a result of Jackson meeting Marceau. It's a technique that mimes use to create the illusion of walking. Jackson introduced it to the world. Anita passed down to me much of what she learned from Marceau, and how he taught her that the chakras could be used to express emotions physically without uttering a single sound. Our bodies as well as our voices must be in alignment to convey our emotions. Marceau says:

> "I have introduced the art of mime to the public. The art which speaks to the soul like music, making comedy and tragedy, involving you, your life, and putting it through the invisible

visible, creating characters, space, making a whole show onstage with our life, our dreams, our expectations."

I am now going to let you in on the secret he shared with so many brilliant performers. Let's start. The three chakras, or energy points, I am focusing on are the brow/third eye, the heart, and the sacral root.

THE THIRD-EYE CHAKRA is located a little above your eyebrows. It represents insight, intuition, wisdom, intelligence, and psychic development.

THE HEART CHAKRA is located in the center of your chest and represents unconditional love, nurturing, and compassion.

THE SACRAL CHAKRA is located between your hips and represents manifestation, sexuality, and emotional connection to others.

The body emulates energy. Have you ever been around someone whose electricity you can feel? Their presence is a very strong one. The same energy can be tapped into when using the chakras and applying them to your stage presence and charisma. If you focus on these energy points, it allows you to use your body in ways you are normally unaware of. And who would ever think about performance and using one's chakras? Dancers, mimes, actors, and now you. Take a look below for examples.

© TDC PHOTOGRAPHY

The Third-Eye Chakra: the Intellect

Have you ever noticed a lawyer, or parent, or someone in an emotional state, trying to convey an important message? They lean in with their head when talking to you. Sometimes this is even accompanied by a pointed finger. Think about a time when you were really trying to convince someone—whether you were upset, or feeling truly passionate about something, or simply trying to sway someone's opinion. You most likely leaned in with your head and your body, your hands on your hips and with a pointed finger. When singing about something of this nature, let your body do the talking as well. Lean in and focus your energy by using your upper body to physically show the intensity of what you're saying.

The Heart Chakra: the Emotions

When you are heartbroken or in love, you feel it in your chest. That's why it is called "heartache," a strange phenomenon of aching within, a pain pulling down on your chest. With happiness, love, or elation, you feel excitement, butterflies, and rapid heartbeat also in your solar plexus, but with a feeling of energy bursting outward. When singing about happy love, try putting your shoulders back and opening your arms. Surrender your body and feel the energy force from your heart by releasing joy and filling up the room; think outside of your body. When you are singing about loss, sadness, or unrequited love, you can touch your heart and breath in—feel the pull and the internal ache. This is so powerful that you may find yourself getting emotional just from the physical memories.

The Sacral Chakra: the Sexual

When you feel confident, flirtatious, or sexy, you walk with a swing and stand with invitation. You seduce and glide, strut, titillate, captivate, and have a sense of place and power. Your energies are focused in the sacral chakra. So when you are singing a song about a passionate night, use your body to impart that feeling: swing your hips, pace the stage, arouse your subject and the audience.

© GLEN JONES

Planting Your Feet

One of the most important parts of performance is the ability to plant your feet. I call it "grounding." You need to ground yourself to maintain balance. Use your feet for energy. Your feet support you in many ways, diaphragmatically for breath control and projection in order to sustain your voice throughout a concert. You also need to plant your feet to command power, energy, and attention onstage. Use the floor, the stage, and the earth as an energy source to support you from the ground up. You'll also notice that many performers bend their knees, plant their feet to allow all the energies to flow through their bodies and chakras and give them vocal power.

Practice the following: Try pairing these lines with physical movements.

USE YOUR THIRD-EYE CHAKRA: Look in the mirror. Lean your head in, point your finger, and sing a song similar to "You Ought to Know," by Alanis Morisette, or "Before He Cheats," by Carrie Underwood.

USE YOUR HEART CHAKRA: Look in the mirror. Open your arms to your sides, look up to the sky, the ceiling, and the lights and sing a song similar to "Without You," originally sung by Bad Finger and later covered by Mariah Carey. You can even touch your heart and look at yourself in the mirror. Or, for a happy love song, sing "Just the Way You Are," by Bruno Mars, or "I'm Yours," by Jason Mraz, or a song of your choice.

THE SACRAL CHAKRA: Look in the mirror and slide your hands up and down the sides of your hips. Stand in a flirtatious position and think about someone you are attracted to. Sing a song of your choice with the same emotion as Michael Jackson's "The Way You Make Me Feel" or Robin Thicke's "Lost Without You."

This chapter has visual examples on the DVD that comes with this book. Please refer to it for more insight.

PART II

DRESS REHEARSAL

5

DESIGNING YOUR SET

WHAT DO YOUR SONGS SAY ABOUT YOU?

"Music washes away from the soul the dust of everyday life."
—RED AUERBACH

Performing your songs well is one thing, but putting together a show is another thing all together. It often happens alongside promoting a new CD: you want to share your new songs with an audience in the hope that they will enjoy them, come back again, and buy them. When designing a set, there are many elements to focus on. Having a theme is always a good idea. The most famous artists and tours all have themes. Think of your set as being made up of snapshots of an artist's life—framed, captioned, and paired with a new collection of songs, much like a painter's exhibit in a gallery. Everyone is invited to participate in an entertaining night. Each exhibit has its own flavor, and you get better with each show.

So what kind of event do you want to design for your latest song collection? Keep in mind that chapters 5 through 8 are going to take you through a series of elements that you can use when putting on a live show. In this chapter, I am focusing on the theme of your show, your song choice, and the venue. Let's start by looking at some famous tours and their show ideas.

- Singer-songwriter Sarah McLachlan's tour in 2010 was called Sarah and Friends. This interactive tour consisted of an intimate setting, with Sarah sitting and singing songs with guest performers. The audience got the opportunity to submit questions to their favorite singers and hear them give *up-close and personal responses* to them. It was the first tour of its kind.

- Pop icon Beyoncé's tour in 2009, called the I Am Sasha Fierce Tour, was showcasing Beyoncé's alter ego. This tour took eight months of rehearsing, stage planning, and costume design to show the *metamorphosis of Beyoncé into Sasha Fierce*. Thierry Mugler, a French fashion designer, wanted to fulfill the singer's vision by designing outfits that were feminine, free, and warriorlike. Beyoncé performed more than 104 shows on six continents.

- Cultural musician Kid Rock's Born Free Tour is in honor of the troops. It's a tribute to their sacrifices, their selflessness, and their tireless service in defense of the United States. The songs and concert showcase his obsession with all things red, white, and blue, and his love is muscle cars, hip-hop music, country rock, getting drunk on lakes in northern Michigan—he's in love with them all, and fashions melding them together. Kid says, "I was on one of my trips to Afghanistan and Iraq, playing for our troops, and I started to just think about no matter where somebody was born in this world, how lucky you are just by the grace of God to be born free."

- Beatles band member Paul McCartney, in his 2004 U.S. Tour, created *a circus theme*. I got a chance to see my all-time hero in person at the Staples Center in Los Angeles. A giant-size beach ball was bounced around the arena by the audience members themselves, and men on 20-foot stilts, jugglers, and unicyclists blended together amid colorful streamers in an atmosphere of fun and frolic. Much like his musical hits from the past 40 years, not one song was unrecognizable. His upright piano was painted in rainbows, and a backdrop that looked like the battleship game board lit up with multicolored pegs. Two hours and 45 minutes and three encores later, we all left with our lives having been replayed, and our hearts filled to the brim. It was pure magic!

- The magician Michael Jackson's summer 2010 This Is It Tour never materialized due to his tragic death, but it was still one of the most anticipated shows in history. We were all able to view the rehearsal tapes and follow him behind the scenes in the movie *This Is It*, as he prepared for the tour launch. The extravagant lights, green screen special effects, and 3-D experience would have been one of a kind. Michael's theme was the *delicate future of our planet*, and his dream of achieving peace and love between all mankind.

Each of these tours had unique artists of specific genres and unique themes, from up-close and personal, to a feminist metamorphosis, to a high-tech 3-D look at our delicate planet, to a fun and happy-go-lucky circus theme. I'm aware that most of us don't have the budgets or global fame to go on a world tour. You're most likely looking at booking a gig in a local club. Still, closing your eyes and envisioning yourself performing onstage can then be played out in a more simplified rendition. After all, why edit yourself and your vision? I also suggest watching your favorite artists live on YouTube. What do you like about their shows? What parts of their shows can you realistically incorporate into your own? Also, flip back to chapter 2 and revisit your Meyers-Briggs type result and worksheet for inspiration. See if any of it sparks some ideas. When you put together your setlist of songs, is there a connective story between each one? Do the song titles themselves help depict a theme? Do they paint a picture, or perhaps create a mood for the night? There is a lot that one can do to create interesting visuals and experiences. Consider the audience experience. Could you perhaps have something for everyone in the audience, so you can invite them to partici-pate with you during the show? Hand them glow sticks so they can wave all together at one point, or get them to sing along with you?

Could you have your background singers sitting among the audience before coming up to sing—an element of surprise? And, what can you do for visuals onstage? I'll talk about fashion later in the book, but what about a look for the stage itself? Christmas lights are easy to wrap around your instruments or mic stands. Light sets can be purchased that are triggered by your drummer's kick pedal in rhythm. Plugging in a portable fan to blow your hair, or scarves, or streamers can have a cool effect. Hanging art off of your instruments can add an interesting element. Your goal is to stand out from an oversaturation of performances. It begins with the audience members' experience as they enter the room, then continues through the show itself, and then affects what they are leaving with. So much can be done to create a wonderful evening with imagination on an affordable budget.

Things You Can Do

Create a strong introduction to your show.
Make sure that songs blend together.
Consider tempo, key, and instrumentation.
Create a buildup, or breakdown, at a pivotal moment in the show.
Put one cover song in your set and put your own spin on it.
Make sure that your finale leaves the audience in the palm of your hand.

OPENING AND INTRODUCTION. Do something uniquely you. How are you bringing the audience into your world? Are you starting with a huge opener? Or are you coming out rather raw and building from there. I once saw a John Mayer concert in which John opened for himself by doing an acoustic set. He strolled onstage in torn-up jeans, a T-shirt, and a baseball cap. The lights in the stadium were still on, and he appeared to be a stagehand—tuning the guitars and fiddling with the cables and the mic stand without any announcement or anyone paying much attention at all. Suddenly he sat down and started playing. He didn't even lift his head to let us see his face. It took the audience awhile to realize who it was, and when he started to sing they went wild! So one can be creative in the way they choose to open a show at any level.

SONGS SHOULD WORK WELL TOGETHER. Keep in mind that all your tempos, song topics, and keys you are performing in should be well thought out. Song choice is important. We all know Enya and her signature sound. Her show is a night of haunting, angelic-sounding music. If you were designing her setlist, however, what would you need to look out for? As beautiful as her ballads may be in concert, they can become predictable and boring if the entire show is too much the same. A show needs some relief or pivotal moment, changes of timbre to carry us along. Looking at the opposite end of the spectrum, the band Megadeth gives its audience and 45 minutes of heavy, hard-hitting, nonstop music. That won't keep the audience's attention the entire time, either. Weave in a blend of music that will carry your listeners along with you. The use of varying dynamics, moods, and subject matter needs to be present to keep your set moving and alive. Make sure that the songs you've written in the same key are not played back-to-back. And it's important that every song is not about unrequited love, or hating the world, or how you think you're "all that." Personally, I think that quiet moments onstage can be extremely memorable and powerful, especially following a dramatic number. Just you, the words, one instrument, and the chance for you to let us in. Do you remember the saying "If you want to capture someone's attention, whisper?" Try it sometime. Start whispering on the phone to a friend, and they will whisper back instantly and mimic you. It's funny! Also, everyone else wants to hear what you're whispering. When a person speaks quietly, everyone leans in to hear what he or she has to say. Don't forget to have that shared moment in your set, the same way you have a moment when the entire room is tapping and clapping and singing along.

RECOGNIZABLE FACTOR. When you're just starting out, no one really knows your songs. Perhaps a few avid fans, such as your mom, know your material, but many people in the room are hearing it for the first time. When looking over your setlist, try to find a place for a cover tune. That can be a nice surprise for the audience. If you are shy a song or two, you can use cover songs to fill in the spots. And be sure to rearrange a cover song to fit your style, your voice, and your genre—and give it a twist. You can have a lot of fun with song choices. I had a student, a male Tori Amos–type of artist, sit at the piano and perform a rendition of Britney Spears's "Oops! . . . I Did it Again" in a minor key with distorted guitars, making it dark and dingy. It was awesome!

CREATE A BUILDUP TO A PIVOTAL MOMENT IN THE SHOW. Think about designing your setlist in an arc shape by splitting it into sections. There are usually seven or eight songs in a 45-minute set.

Opening ◆ 2 songs ◆ Pivotal Moment ◆ 2 songs ◆ Finale ◆ Encore

Let your songs do the talking by creating your theme. How will you open the night? I say something exciting, capturing the attention of the audience and playing straight through until the third song. You can then talk a bit. The third, fourth, and fifth songs are crucial in the set. That's where many shows lose momentum. Everyone usually has great ideas for opening and closing the show. A big ending equals big applause. So how to keep the flow throughout the middle? I say, use dynamics. Take a look at some suggestions I have for tempos and some set layouts. A pivotal moment in your show could be the slow buildup to one big up-tempo number if you are a mellow artist. Or if you're a high-energy act with an evening of intensity, your pivotal moment could be something heartfelt, vulnerable, and mellow. You can use anything that leads to a peak moment and back—a twist of events, or a surprise of some sort, before taking us home.

High-Energy Act

UP-TEMPO—UP-TEMPO, MIDTEMPO, ACOUSTIC, MIDTEMPO COVER, UP-TEM-PO, UP-TEMPO, FINALE I also would like to point out that a set does not have to be eight songs; in fact, it's often better to leave your audience wanting more. And it depends on the show itself and the length of your songs. So keep that in mind when designing your setlist. Think about how long you can keep the momentum going, and when it starts to feel as though you're losing the edge, make your set shorter.

Some of you may be saying, "But I am a mellower artist. What do I do to keep the audience interested for eight songs?" I say that instrumentation has a lot to do with keeping a show interesting. Your midtempo songs can feel more energy-driven by using players, and your ballads performed solo become the quiet and intimate moments in your set. I would make sure that whatever cover you choose has more energy than all the other songs, and that you use that as your high point or pivotal moment of your show.

Mellower Act

MELLOW—MIDTEMPO, MIDTEMPO, UP-TEMPO COVER, SOLO, MIDTEMPO, MIDTEMPO, SOLO Consider adding cajon, cello, percussion, mandolin, flute, stand-up bass, and background vocals. Any of these instruments will add texture to your set, your sound, and the intensity of your songs. Mellower songs would use fewer instruments, and I suggest you have everyone leave the stage when you sing solo. This way, the audience will feel that the show has variety.

If you are a soloist, perhaps do what KT Tunstall does with a loop pedal, creating textures and layers. Or play a couple of songs with your laptop and instrumental tracks, or drum loops and grooves.

If you are a folk artist and a purist doing the coffeehouse circuit—just you and a guitar—the next chapter will help. In this case, your stories will carry your show. In fact, every artist should be able to deliver a full set and an unplugged set, in order to be a better performer.

DON'T OVERSTAY YOUR WELCOME. Don't be the no-hint person. There's nothing worse than someone who doesn't know when to get off the stage. You can't cram 12 songs into 45 minutes, or continue to do encore after encore. Short and sweet works. How many times have you seen a movie trailer that showed everything that was going to happen in the movie, so there was no point in going. You may lose your audience for your next show if you are the last to leave the party. As a performer, you have to read the room and know when to pass the microphone on to the next act!

GO TO THE VENUE BEFORE THE NIGHT OF YOUR SHOW. Check out the size of the stage, the backline (stage monitors, any instruments, sound equipment) provided, if any. Check out the lighting and the kind of audience that is drawn to this type of venue. (If you're not quite sure what to look for or request, I will cover more of the technical aspects in chapter 8.) Watch what is and isn't working while other bands perform. All of these elements are going to affect how you plan on performing in that room, and what will and won't work when you put on your show. Even if ideas you have are too big for this particular venue, keep working on different ways to open and close your shows for a variety of spaces. This will keep you and your act spontaneous and creative. And be willing to try different things. Some of them may work and others may not, but live performance is all about learning on the job.

In the end, you'll know which songs are the strongest from performing them live. You'll be able to try your sets out and find what is and isn't working. Until then, think opening, middle, and closer to keep the arc of the show flowing. Leave the audience with either a high-energy, happy feeling, or an intimate moment of thought. Before your last song, thank the audience for supporting you, and keep them engaged by talking about another show. Here are some interesting options: have a friend film the show and interview people as they enter the venue to see you perform. Tell them that they can watch the footage later online and see how their participation made your performance so much better. You can tell friends and fans to meet you afterward, where they can have their picture taken with you, and then it will be uploaded instantly to your website. Do anything different that keeps concertgoers involved in the process by personalizing their experience. And don't forget to mention the next band coming up! Be visible following the show. And no matter what, thank people if they compliment you. One big lesson I learned after someone came backstage to talk to me on a night I thought I had done terribly. I came across as though I were ungrateful. Don't make excuses if you didn't like your performance. It's as if someone were to say, "You look good today!" And you say, "No, I don't—I look terrible. I'm tired, I hate my outfit, bla, bla, bla." All that does is make the person who complimented you feel stupid. If a fan liked your show, thank them.

Take a moment to think about the kind of show you'd like to produce. Think of a theme, the list of songs you will sing, the arc of your set. Consider special visuals you can add onstage and any experience that is different for audience members to remember you by. And, of course, any merchandise or special give-aways you can offer is always a plus. Now take all of these ideas and fill out the questionnaire below.

Designing Your Set

What's your theme? Your inspiration?

_____
_____
_____
_____
_____
_____
_____
_____
_____
_____

How are you opening your show? Anything unique about it?

_____
_____
_____
_____
_____
_____
_____
_____
_____

Create a setlist of songs that will take your audience on a journey.

1. _____
2. _____
3. _____
4. _____

5. _____

6. _____

7. _____

8. _____

What cover song will you do? Make sure to revamp it to fit your musical genre. What kind of spin are you putting on the song? (For example, one of my students did a country version of Lady Gaga's "Speechless," with a train groove and slide guitar—pretty different!)

_____

_____

_____

_____

_____

_____

_____

What's the pivotal moment?

_____

_____

_____

_____

_____

_____

What's your finale?

_____

_____

_____

_____

_____

_____

_____

_____

_____

NOTES

6

BETWEEN THE MUSIC

STORIES AND ANECDOTES

"Music is nothing separate from me. It is me . . .
You'd have to remove the music surgically."
—RAY CHARLES

Now that you've thought about songs, show themes and visuals, let's talk about connecting the invisible threads that exist between the music.

CHEESY CLICHÉS. I love cheese on a cracker with a nice glass of red wine. Not onstage. How many times have you heard this? "Hey there everybody, how y'all doing? What's up! I can't hear you. Make some noise. Come on and make some noise. Throw your hands in the air." All the clichés that have the same ring of a bad pickup line from someone you don't want to date in a dingy bar. It seems as if every singer on the planet has bought the "Say This at Your Next Gig" handbook. All the excitement and personality is taken out of you and your show with this predictable audience banter. There are so many more creative ways to introduce yourself and your songs, talk to the audience, and keep your show fresh.

THE AUDIENCE KNOWS MORE THAN YOU THINK. There's no need to explain everything to your audience. You don't do that in everyday life—you simply are "in the moment." Imagine meeting someone for the first time at a social event, and they say to you:

> "Hi. I'm Bill, and I just wanted to let you know that I'm going to talk to you now and tell you a story. I'm going to describe events that have taken place in my life that are funny, and you're

going to laugh, right? What? I can't hear you. Tell me you're going to laugh."

Hmmm. Wouldn't that be strange to actually meet someone who acted like that? Well, that's what inexperienced performers often sound like onstage. They mark their every move, tell us what they are going to do, and then tell us how to react. The audience knows it's a song you are about to play, and that you most likely wrote it. And one more thing, I like to have my own interpretations of some songs, and feel it as I will. Many songs have been written that have nothing to do with what the general audience thinks they're about. The beauty of music is what each individual experiences. If you tell your listeners everything about every single song, there's no room left for individual interpretation. It's TMI—too much information—and the set becomes claustrophobic. I saw one guy who talked between every song and told us all about each one of them. Here's an example I personally witnessed:

> "So, this next song is about my dead grandfather. He was not very nice to me or anybody. But a funny thing happens once people die—you forgive them. I feel really sorry for my grand-mother now that she's alone. She's probably a lot happier, but I'm gonna sing this song I wrote even though she's not really fond of it. I guess because I tell it like I see it. It's called 'Now That You're Gone.'"

Okay, so now I know too much. I don't like the grandfather, who the song's about. This guy's poor grandmother doesn't even like the song he wrote for her. Maybe it's not that good. All this noise in my head that has nothing to do with how I may have felt about the song if I had been able to experience it on my own. The artist warned me how to feel all night long.

WHAT YOU SAY BETWEEN SONGS SHOULD ALL BE PART OF A CONVERSATION. When you talk to your audience, make sure to bring them in on the experience. A better way to introduce a song might be to tell them about your travels and how you ended up at the club that night—as though they have an inside scoop on what's happening around you, and your take on it. The people who come to hear you don't want to feel that they are one of the millions you talk to about your work. They would rather feel that they're in on knowing you more intimately. Think of anecdotes and stories that relate to the message of the songs you will be performing, without saying "and so

I wrote this song," or "and so here's the song." An interesting introduction could be simply playing your instrument while saying something like, "On my way over tonight, I stopped off at a great little shop for coffee on Beverly Boulevard—you may have heard of it, Coffee Roasters. I was sitting there and I overheard this young couple next to me talking about their first trip back home. And how strange it's going to be going back for the first time in years. I know we've all been there." Then just start singing the song:

> *Too many years have come and gone far,*
> *Dreams of forever to get where we are.*
> *If I could fold time and my body in half,*
> *I'd run through the alleys, the breeze, and the grass.*
> *Oh those memories are tall as small as I stood,*
> *Inside this house of concrete and wood*
> *From my childhood.*

So the song itself finishes the conversation. There's a seamless transition before, during, and after. You've made the audience members feel as though they are part of the experience by referencing a local place in their home-town that they might know, and you've tied it all together in a magical way.

If you're doing a cover song (for example, "Billionaire," by Travie Mc-Coy and featuring Bruno Mars), you might talk about how you can't believe that in a world as rich as ours, there could be even one hungry person. Say something to make the crowd think, and something to make the song stand out on its own and have an impactful meaning.

> *Yeah I would have a show like Oprah.*
> *I would be the host of Everyday Christmas*
> *Give Travie a wish list, pull an Angelina and Brad Pitt,*
> *Adopt a bunch of babies that ain't never had sh-t,*
> *Give away a few Mercedes like, "Here lady, have this,"*
> *And last but not least, grant somebody their last wish.*
> *I'd probably visit where Katrina hit,*
> *Do a lot more than FEMA did.*

Let's apply this idea to different categories, because you are all not singer-songwriters. Let's talk about Lady Gaga—a Pop Icon performer, an alter ego. Her character talks as the leader of her "Little Monsters" who em-power her, and she in turn gives them back their power. Here's an excerpt of one of her live shows:

"Tonight when you leave the monster ball, leave not loving me more—leave loving yourself more because you are a superstar and you were born that way. I want you to forget all of your insecurities, let go of any person who ever made you feel bad about who you are, or made you feel insecure, not wanted, or that you could never be anything great, or they talked down to you or made you feel small. I want you to let go of it all, because I used to be in the audience looking at some—on the stage that I wanted to be on. And I promised myself that when I got up here one day that I would be much more grateful then she was."

Stefani Joanne Angelina Germanotta brilliantly designed her infamous Lady Gaga persona. That's not necessarily who she is at home after the show. Alice Cooper plays the part of the villain who keeps coming back time and time again! Dolly Parton talks about how much of a country girl she is, and how she came from a poor family, but how her mama cooked and sewed and loved with all her heart. A hip-hop artist has a hype man bring him up and out! There are so many different ways to address the audience with each approach. What will you say?

KEEPING THE FLOW. There's no need to stop between every song to talk to the audience. That's too much like "granny stops," driving in the car and constantly pumping the brake. Once you've got a good momentum going musically, take your listeners on a ride. They don't need explanations or stories between every song; pick your points when you talk and let the music do the rest. I often like to connect the first and second song by a musical transition and not speak until the third song. That gives the audience a chance to see you, hear you, and let you in. These musical transitions can add personality as well.

DON'T DROP THE ENERGY BETWEEN SONGS. One of the most important elements for a performer is not to relax too much in between songs or during transitions. The show is not over when you're not playing or singing— you're still onstage. Stay in the moment, and keep your focus. Also, please don't grab a giant plastic bottle of water and suck the pacifier end of it as if we're at a pit stop. Put your water in a glass—that's much more appealing then jugging a big old baby bottle of designer water. You can take a drink when the music features your guitarist or piano player, or perhaps even a percussion solo. I suggest designing a couple of places when you can catch

your breath in your set. Plan it out with the band if you have a highly en-
ergetic show.

IT'S A MICROPHONE, NOT A LOLLIPOP. A lot of singers hold the microphone
so close to their mouth that they become inaudible, even distorted, and you
can't hear them and can't see their mouth in the event that you have to lip-
read. During soundcheck have somebody let you know when you can be
heard in the room. Ask one of your bandmates to listen from off stage and
let you know when the volume is good. That way you don't have to eat the
mic to be heard.

THE MIC STAND. Once you remove the microphone from the mic stand, also
move the mic stand out of the way. Simply moving to the right or left of it
and continuing to sing does not fix the problem. It feels as though something is not complete. And it's an eyesore, taking up space and energy. Take
the stand and place it behind you or to one side of the drum kit, so everyone
can be seen. Now the stage has moving room, and you're not being blocked
or upstaged by a long, skinny, lonely black pole.

ALWAYS CROSS THE STAGE WITH AN INTENTION. There must be a reason
for your movement onstage. If I were talking to you in real life and all of
a sudden I walked away in midsentence, it would feel awkward. If you are
crossing to one side of the stage, have an intention. Pick someone out of the
audience and cross over to them to sing to them or to tell them your story.
Or tell that side of the room what it is you want them to know. It's much
more effective. Use right, left, and center stage as planting points to move
from so that the entire audience is able to see you throughout your performance. Don't forget the balcony if there is one, the last rows, and your
band. Be sure to include everyone, and look at your players, the drummer,
the backup vocalists—all the people on the stage. And introduce those who
are helping to make your show a success.

Let it all flow between the music, your stories, your transitions between
songs, and your stage movements and the center space you create. Keep
all these things I have discussed in mind. You are the lead vocalist and the
focal point of the set—the lighthouse calling all ships to shore in the night.

This chapter has visual examples in the DVD. Please refer to it for more
insight.

7

FINDING YOUR FASHION MUSE

SHOPPING IN YOUR CLOSET

"You are the music while the music lasts."
—T. S. Eliot

Fashion and music are two worlds intertwined. A group's music and lyric can entice many to crave their sounds, their energy, their look. Rock icons have inspired fashion designers to develop a look capturing the essence of their music. It has become a collaboration between composers, poets, and fashion maestros—all painting the canvas of an artist's image. From David Bowie and Gucci to Madonna and Jean Paul Gaultier, and from Haute Couture to the newly inspired Jimi Hendrix Collection by Rock and Roll Religion, the design world and musicians fuse together. And Lady Gaga's attire continues to create "shock and awe" for both the media and audiences. Whether it is a rough 'n' tumble, a classic 'n' cool, or a risqué 'n' tantalizing image you choose, make it your own. Fashions change hourly and I love glamour and high fashion, but on a musician's budget, many of us don't have the means or luxury to shop at the finest places and/or have our own stylist to help us pick out our look for each show. To feel as though I have something new, I shop in my closet and try pairing things together I normally wouldn't. Why is it that on Halloween we have complete permission to dress anyway we like? Keep that thought in mind when considering a style for the next night you are performing. Michael Jackson monopolized on that with *Thriller*. Creating your own fashions by using accessories to enhance your look onstage is always an option. Garments that are timeless are a good investment and allow you to accessorize with what I call "fashion spotlights"—something that stands out. Remember that you are a performer. Even if you are singing in a local coffee house, something about you must be unique and different from the "normal" everyday person. You might want to define what "unique" is for you, based on your music and personality. Is it Celine Dion/Carrie Underwood glamorous, Gwen Stefani/Elvis Costello quirky, Katie Perry/Elton John bubbly fun, Lady Gaga/David Bowie artsy and strange, Pink/Foo Fighters sporty, Madonna/Justin Timberlake sexy, Black Eyed Peas/Michael Jackson futuristic, or Aerosmith/Kid Rock gritty rock 'n' roll? There are many ways to go, and those I've mentioned have strong, memorable, personalized, or even branded images.

Most of us never knew what a stylist was until the industry revealed a look "behind the scenes" on television shows. These are professionals hired by record labels, movie houses, and print and magazine companies to buy clothes and dress their subjects. I had the wonderful opportunity to get some inside tips to share with you from two stylists in the industry. First, I spoke to Manuel Benecides, who styles hair, is a makeup artist, and has styled many rock stars for the Grammy Awards. Manuel has worked with Prince, Bob Dylan, Beyoncé and Destiny's Child, Kelly Moneymaker (of Exposé), Jane Seymour, cast members of the TV series *Scrubs*, to name a few. We spoke about style and fashion.

Q: How did you enter into the world of fashion and beauty?

A: It's the old Hollywood story: I met somebody who was a stylist, and I started going out on jobs assisting them. I thought, "Wow, this is what I want to do." So I sold my business in New York, moved out here to Los Angeles, and the rest just fell into place. I became part of the *Glam Squad*—you'll hear that term a lot on the red carpet. I became one of the team members who gets to style, beautify, and serve people.

Q: Most people don't know how important stylists are in helping an artist find their "look." That takes a special talent. How do you help artists define or design a unique look?

A: I always say, it is essentially up to you. You've got to know who you are, know what you like or don't like, and we can create your look that matches your personality. And it's important to take into account what is the message you're trying to say with your music.

Q: What is the area in which most people miss their mark?

A: Most people miss the mark if they try to be trendy. Many artists are trying to ride the wave, and think they are being current. Also, what works in a club, doesn't necessarily translate onstage. And keep in mind that everything that is on the runways in Paris now will be hot here in the States in two years. To Thine Own Self Be True is my motto. Steven Tyler hasn't changed his look in 30 years, and yet it's relevant every time he shows up. Stevie Nicks still wears those black lacey dresses and high boots, but without that look, she couldn't spin around and do her Stevie Nicks' thing. People who are individuals, people of that "ilk," don't care what everybody else is doing. There's only one Pink, one Cher, one Madonna, one Lady Gaga.

Q: What would you suggest for an artist who is striving to have that "star look"?

A: I don't want people to get disappointed thinking they can do it all on their own. Some of us have an eye and talent for putting a look together. Take LeAnn Rimes when she first started out, compared to once she got a team of stylists. Now she's showing up on the Red Carpet as a *glamozon*. It takes a team of people to be like the stars: someone has dressed you, someone has made you up, someone is controlling your voice onstage, someone has the lighting perfect, and on and on—that is the biggest thing to think about. There are teams of people helping these high-end artists. You can't try to compete with that, but you can perhaps work with people coming up in the business by finding assistants to a big stylist. And there are also a lot of shows on television that show you how to do this kind of stuff.

Q: What do you tell musicians who are out there on their own, just starting out with a dollar budget?

A: Thrift shops are great. These days places such as Crossroads, and others, carry previously owned or lightly worn clothing. They don't carry clothes that aren't relevant. You can go there and get a high-end pair of jeans for $30 that were $300 at Barneys New York. Pair it up with a vintage coat over a 1960's Vegas shirt with piping, with really cool buttons and cards on the shoulder, and it looks great. Take ideas and mix them up and create your own style. The same thing applies for women. You can even ask a friend who always look good to help you shop.

Q: Who have you worked with that you love?

A: I've worked with so many wonderful people. But there's an 11-year-old boy, who I've been styling since he was 4. He's like a nephew to me. It's not about the "stars"; it's about my clients who end up being family to me, like Kelly Moneymaker has become family.

Q: What are you working on now that is exciting?

A: I'm working on Germany's next top model with Heidi Klum. It's high-end fashion this time, and very exciting!

Q: Any last words of wisdom?
A: Remember not to take it all so seriously. Have fun. We are here on this planet to serve, to teach and help each other through life. It's quite humbling when you think about it.

Whatever you decide to do, it's all valuable advice on Manuel's part and a good inside look at the entertainment world. I even had Ken Pavés do my hair when he was up-and-coming in the industry. So, you never know who you may get to work with! I got to work with Cat Winnekamp and invited her as a guest stylist to one of my classes. I was intrigued by Cat, who has lived and worked in London, New York, and Los Angeles, giving her an international perspective on music and fashion. She has accessorized backdrops for photo shoots of models in high-fashion magazines and dressed musicians in music videos, and her creative taste and vision is influenced by her international travels and her love of foreign films and music. Some of her clients include Malin Akerman, Lydia Hearst, Lloyd, Damian Marley, Bruno Mars, Shemar Moore, Nas, Kate Nash, Edgar Ramirez, Sleigh Bells, and Odette Yustman.

Q: Tell us about yourself, and what drew you into fashion?
A: I was born in Los Angeles, and then had the great opportunity to live and travel in Europe and the East Coast. As a result of this exposure, I was greatly influenced by multiple cultures and styles. I have always had a passion for creating, sewing, or reconstructing my own clothes since I was little. As I grew older, it became clear that my passion for fashion styling would be the road I would travel. I was fortunate enough to be able to assist celebrity stylists and photographers, and with this positive experience I not only knew I had found my dream job, but wanted to make my all my clients look the best they possibly could.

Q: You've lived in London and have a love for foreign films. Having worked in high-end fashion and styling musicians, what's the difference between Europe and America?
A: Where the difference lies is fashion in Europe is more daring and outrageous. But then in the States our music labels are larger, our artists are more powerful, and their style is more copied than any well-known European fashion magazine. While walking the streets in America you can see

the strong European influence in our fashion, and the things we choose to represent ourselves on the exterior. And on the opposite end of the spectrum, while living in Europe everywhere you go you hear American songs. In London, whether it's the driver in a taxi cab bobbing his head to a new Jay-Z song, a new club or discotheque playing the latest Lady Gaga song, or an English Pub where they are playing American rock 'n' roll songs, you hear it everywhere. So in essence there lies a synergistic trend where the music industry takes style inspiration from Europe, and Europe takes music inspiration from the States.

Q: I believe the pendulum swings with fashion and music, and we've recently gone from a laid-back look to having fun again with "showmanship" and "fantasy." Lady Gaga's an example and a throwback to the days of David Bowie and Madonna, pushing the envelope. Are more people following that trend, or is everyone different? What would you suggest for each client?

A: I would tell each client that my goal is to help them achieve their own fantasy look, preferably, an amped-up version of themselves. Whether it is as simple as wearing all black and creating a dark and mysterious look, or as extreme as a getup Lady Gaga would wear. The artists have to feel comfortable in their own skin and as well give off a sense of personal style and pride to their fans and audiences. It's so important to remember that as a musician, you are living out the fantasy that millions of other people have. You are an escape, a source of happiness and enjoyment with a multitude of emotions, and your exterior should convey your passion to your audience.

Q: Who are some of the fashion trendsetters of today that we may not know about?

A: There are so many fashion trendsetters that are unknown to the general public, who dress just as extreme as Lady Gaga and are just as daring. To name a few: socialite and heir to the Guinness beer fortune, Daphne Guinness; Editor of Vogue Nippon, Anna Dello Russo; and even Bjork, the extreme electronic artist from Iceland who made headlines in her infamous swan dress. Even now Bjork seems tame compared to the likes of Nicki Minaj and Lady Gaga. MGMT is an all male, up-and-coming, new-wave band. Their style is loud, bold, and is very reminiscent to the extreme styles of David Bowie and Steven Tyler. They are great examples of men in the music industry pushing the limits in fashion and pulling it off with flying colors.

Q. How can one, as you say, "amp up" their outfit on a low budget?

A: Anything in your closet can be transformed to create a unique embellishment or be a subtle statement. Take a scarf you have and tie it around your neck for a retro or vintage look. Or wrap it around your hips for a more rocker '70s look. Take shoes—whether high heels, flats, or Converses—and spray-paint them metallic or a bright color. Depending on the material of the shoe, it will soak up the spray-paint differently—so try to remember it will achieve a chic look on patent leather shoes and a grungy look on shoes with a clothlike material like canvas. If a more glamorous "va va voom" Katy Perry/Beyoncé look is what you're trying to achieve, then purchase some sequins at a local arts-and-crafts store, and sew as many as you can onto a bra or tight-fitting top. This may take some time, but the result will be worth it and have cost you a few bucks! And lastly, if you're on an extremely tight budget and you're a more laid-back musician, I highly recommend going to your local vintage store and sorting through their clothes, which span every decade from the 20th century for men and women. You're guaranteed to find an original yet easy look.

Q. Any secrets you'd like to share?

A: I always try to style my clients with clothes that not only complement their skin tone, hair color, and body type but their overall vibe. That may not be a secret to some, but definitely is helpful when putting outfits together. A bigger stylist secret is definitely using double-stick tape for your clothes. This allows for the musician to wear more daring things, while ensuring no "boob slippage" or wardrobe malfunctions! And lastly, use Google! I look up photos of inspiration for my clients from magazines to musicians to celebrities, by searching anything and everything that inspires me. Make it personal. Look up who you enjoy watching and listening to and hearing. See how they represent themselves and try to emulate that with your own twist.

Q. Any favorite stories behind the scenes?

A: I have so many stories that it's hard to choose! The juicy ones I have to leave out, unfortunately, but I do fondly remember when I was on set with Daft Punk and we were shooting the promotional add for the TRON: Legacy movie. Daft Punk did the score for the movie, and is probably one of the biggest electronic bands in the world. While on set I was so baffled with how professional and involved they were with the project. They wanted to be a part of every last detail, from lighting to poses to the construction of the set. They weren't just puppets created by the music industry. That's when I could clearly see that all their success had stemmed sheerly from not only their great talent, but also hard work ethic. They cared and wanted it just as badly as they did the first day they started.

My other favorite experience was styling Bruno Mars for his Grenade music video. His energy and amazing talent was endless. He would show me his amazing dance moves in his trailer, and I said, "Why on earth haven't you shown the world these dance skills yet?!" And he says, "I have to ease these dance moves in slowly, I can't show America all my secrets yet!" I really enjoyed his enthusiasm and confidence.

And of course I will never forget styling Damian Marley and rapper Nas's music video. They were both so intimidating at first, but by the end of the shoot, both were teddy bears. They definitely know how to have a good time on set. Sometimes in my job it's hard to remember that it is work, and that's why I am so fortunate and happy to have chosen such an awe-inspiring and creative field.

Perhaps we should all be so lucky to live doing what we passionately love. So when it comes to fashion, take Manuel's and Cat's advice and be true to yourself and create something uniquely you.

Whether you're visiting the local thrift shop, shopping with a friend, mixing and matching and creating your own style—most of all, you'll need to create your "visual aid." What's that? Well, review and think about all the famous singers you love. I guarantee that each one of them has something that you can identify them with. Google images of the following performers, and you'll see what I'm talking about. You can identify a lot of them with their visual aid!

> **MICHAEL JACKSON:** Silver-glitter glove and socks
> **BONO:** Red-tinted glasses
> **THE EDGE:** Beanie cap
> **PINK:** Purple, blonde, pink, blue, magenta hair and more…
> **STEVEN TYLER:** A microphone stand with scarves tied all around it, loose open shirts, and skintight pants
> **JOSS STONE:** Long hippie dresses and bare feet
> **LADY GAGA:** Anything goes!

Decide what your visual aid is going to be; it should be something that your audience can identify you with. You may already wear it every day.

Perhaps it's something you also bring onstage—a certain microphone stand, like country singer Miranda Lambert's, which is made out of a shotgun, or your favorite beat-up acoustic guitar, with a hole in it like folksinger Glen Hansard's, or Tom Waits's vintage microphone. You decide.

DESIGN YOUR OWN FEEL SHEET. Above is an example of a feel sheet I put together for myself. I looked through magazines and online and found pictures of people and outfits that I am attracted to, and then created a feel sheet. This sheet will change, obviously, as styles change, but it's a great tool to figure out what it is that you are into at the time. See what you can find at home or in your closet. Consider the following: pump it up. Take staple pieces—for example, a black dress for women, jeans and a T-shirt for men—and add some flair; a hat, a scarf, a rocking belt, shoes, wild hair, makeup, color accents, zippers, buttons, and different textures of clothing or designs on the fabrics can make simple pieces look glamorous and artsy. Consider how much skin to show.

Color My World

When it comes to colors, be very careful what you pick and choose. Pick rich, vibrant colors and be aware of how they look against your skin. If you are fair skinned like I am, beiges and whites and certain pastels will wash you out. Also, certain colors will bring out your eyes and look good with your hair color and your features. Hopefully, you've been complimented when wearing certain colors, and you have a good instinct. If you're darker skinned, don't wear dark colors that blend into your skin. You want contrast.

BLACK is always a good color to wear, because it is a color of authority and power. It also makes one look much thinner, and is timeless. If you choose to wear black, make sure that you have accents, patterns, and skin showing.

WHITE is good color for olive completions and darker skin. It represents innocence and purity. It goes with everything, and reflects stage lights and color gels. But consider one thing—it can get very dirty.

RED is a definite attention getter. It immediately catches one's eye and represents the color of love, passion, and excitement. I say use red tastefully or as an accent—too much of this color can pull attention away from you.

BLUE is the opposite of red: it brings a calming, serene feeling. This would be a good color to use if your music is more laid back and relaxed, and if you have blue eyes, it can make them pop onstage.

GREEN is a calming, refreshing color and was worn to represent fertility. It also symbolizes wealth. It is a color that is comfortable to the eye because we see it every day in nature. It is safe and inviting.

YELLOW AND GOLD represent optimism and alertness. They can be exciting in all their glitter, and the colors pops onstage.

PURPLE is luxurious, powerful, royal, and spiritual. Depending on the shade, it can be very elegant.

Whichever color you choose, try it on in various lightings and take your picture. See what makes you pop. You want the outfit to frame you, not the other way around. Ask someone you trust to give you some feedback if you don't have a stylist.

PROMOTING OTHERS: MY FAVORITE BAND T-SHIRTS. Wearing a shirt with a logo or another band's name on it is extremely distracting. The majority of my male students at school have worn Led Zeppelin, Pink Floyd, or Beatles T-shirts at one time or another. They have even gone so far as to wear a T-shirt advertising beer or a concert event they've attended. Regardless of what "it" is on your T-shirt, it draws the audience members' eyes away from your face and what you're conveying. I prefer solid-color shirts without any logos. Anything that distracts from you is a no-no. That includes band members outdressing, out-dancing, and upstaging you.

IF IT IS TOO LOUD, TURN IT DOWN. Stripes and checkers and loud patterns are not appealing, and certain lines can flutter, or cause a moiré effect, under stage lights and on camera.

DRESS THE PART. Your outfit must match your genre. It's great to push the envelope, but gold spandex pants, a short top, and thigh-high boots for a country artist is not going to cut it. Make sure that you are dressing the part!

FLOATING-HEAD SYNDROME. Dressing all in black is cool from time to time. But show some skin if you are doing so. Also make sure that the backdrop of your set or stage is not black if you are head to toe in black: you'll look like a floating head and blend into the walls behind you. If you are dressed in all black, use an accent color in your accessories and jewelry.

LADIES—BEWARE OF THE MINISKIRT. Remember that nine out of ten times the stage you are performing on is elevated. That means the people in the front section are looking up at you. You can put two and two together. Your fans are getting a free peekaboo show! I suggest you wear some sporty shorts or opaque tights underneath.

AVOID WEARING BRAND-NEW SHOES. New shoes rock! They can make your entire outfit feel special. However, breaking them in at a performance can be painful and awkward. Wear comfortable shoes. If you are wearing high heels (or, for guys, new boots or shoes), practice in them and break them in. Make sure that the stage is either carpeted or sticky enough that you won't feel the need to hold back on your performance because you're afraid you may slip and fall when performing.

REALITY BODY CHECK. We are a very size-specific society, and this is true especially in the entertainment industry.

And women, unfortunately, are the most scrutinized. So ladies—please be realistic about your body size. Those of you who have a fuller shape should wear something that is flattering to your body size. Don't try to squeeze into something that is too tight, because it will not only be unflattering, but it will also affect your ability to breath effortlessly. Clothing must be flexible for good movement, singing, and self-esteem. And if you are top heavy, it is important to wear good support clothing. Take pictures of yourself in your outfits, videotape yourself performing in it, and see what it looks like.

You move a lot more onstage then when you're just sitting or standing at a party. All of those pictures of models in magazines are still shots. Much of what you see is not wearable. I was literally stapled into an outfit during my photo shoot, to keep it skintight, and there was a five-foot fan blowing my hair. It was a beautiful picture, but I could not move, sing, or perform in it even if I'd wanted to. Remember that photographs and live performances are two different beasts altogether.

Men, the biggest pet peeve I have about your dressing is the "I don't care" look. If you are inviting people to see you perform, take the time to pick out something that looks good and isn't a wrinkly mess, or a plain pair of jeans and worn-out T-shirt. That's so boring.

FASHION SPOTLIGHTS. Accessories are the key! Scarves, buttons on jackets, hats, belts— anything to accent color and design—are great. Men's ties can be used as accents as well. Try anything to juice up your outfit. But make sure that your accessories don't upstage you. And, beware of the "light-house effect," in which what you're wearing reflects the stage lights and blinds the audience.

Mix 'n' Match

WOMEN. Casual bottom, fancy top. Jeans or army pants look great with a dressy top, high heels, and glamorous jewels. Same in reverse: pair silk pants with a T-shirt, or a silk skirt with a denim jacket. Be creative with what you have.

MEN. Guys can do the same: combine suit pants and a T-shirt, or jeans and a suit jacket or suit vest and a dressy top. Hats, ties, watches, shoes, and arm cuffs all add to your overall look.

SOMETHING OLD AND NEW. Visit your local thrift shop and find some cool vintage pieces for your outfit and pair them up with the latest trends.

HAIR AND MAKEUP. Paying attention to this can add a lot to your look. Try different ways to wear your hair and make sure it is not covering your face, so that the audience is able to see your eyes. This same advice goes for when you are wearing a hat: lift the brim up enough so that there's no shadow being cast over your eyes.

LET'S REVIEW THINGS YOU CAN DO. Choose a visual aid, design your own "feel sheet," consider the color of what you're wearing, shop in your closet, and try wearing something old with something new.

8

DESIGNING A SIGNATURE SOUND

YOUR BAND AND YOU

"To study music, we must learn the rules. To create music, we must break them."
—NADIA BOULANGER

J ust the way that it is important to have a visual identity, having an audio
signature is vital as well. As of late, everyone is beginning to sound the
same. So, how can you sound unique and how can you stand out from the
crowd?

 I've spent years in the recording studio
watching producers develop a song from
its inception through the final mastering.
Producing a song is about the mixture of
layered sounds, the spaces in between,
the perfect combination of the two, and
then enough room to feature the lead vocal, a.k.a. the artist. Many people
forget this paradigm when it comes to playing a live show. It's very much
akin to cooking. What are the perfect ingredients and combination? How
much sugar and spice do you add? How can you create a musical flavor
with your instruments? Finding the sound that is uniquely yours takes time.
How do you mix it all together? I grew up in the Mariah Carey and Celine
Dion days when singing was about vocal acrobatics, as if all singers were
doing triple flips fifty feet in the air. They had big voices, riffs, twists, and
turns and huge productions backing them up. I thought this was the only
way to be. I would put on the karaoke machine and try imitating them until
I would turn beet red. When I couldn't sound like them, I felt inadequate.
I did not have their voice, and no matter how many vocal lessons I took,
I never would. And every time I sat at the piano and wrote songs, they
sounded nothing like what was on the radio. I loved Carol King and James

Taylor, so when Sarah McLachlan and Alanis Morissette emerged on the scene, I was ecstatic. They were more my cup of tea and matched the vocal instrument that I was born with. It was a journey that took me a while to understand. I had to find what was right for my voice and my tone, and develop what would enhance my sound. You do too.

MUSICAL UNIQUENESS. Think about your favorite artists. You know immediately who they are, because their voices are distinct and their musical sonic quality recognizable. As in chapter 7 about color and visuals, music and voices also create a palette, a mood, and a vibe. Artists who are able to integrate these qualities are timeless. Today, many performers get eaten up by the moneymaking factory. They are designed and disposed of after their faddish songs run their course. Don't get me wrong—being commercial and accessible to your listeners is important. But at least be uniquely commercial. You can follow the flow only so far, and then you've got to be original. Create your own fad, and be on the cutting edge and ahead of the game. Don't underestimate your audience; they know instantly if you're trying to pull one over on them, and you'll come across as inauthentic. You'll just be chasing the idea. All this is to say that your artistry must not suffer—balance is the key.

KNOWING YOUR VOCAL SIGNATURE. Do you truly know your voice? Where are the warmest, most beautiful tones in your voice? Where are your best belt notes? Are you a hard rocker with a killer falsetto? Are you a beautiful, angelic soprano? Do you know where your golden tones are as a singer? Did you ever sing a song that seems to be the perfect vocal fit? When you truly know your voice and its unique texture, and marry it with the right songs, the fuller rich tones of your voice are showcased. Your vowels, rhythmic flow, and rare nuances shine, and singing feels effortless! Whether the song's your original composition or a cover, you'll know where you truly belong when it happens, and begin developing your style as a result. Consider the key you are singing in, and practice songs in different keys, or until it feels right. A recording machine doesn't lie, and listening back to what you record will give you a chance to hear how you sound. Listen from another room to your rehearsals or originals. What flavors have you added to your vocal style? What emotion are you getting across? One important note: a lot of people sing with a crying tone throughout the entire song, thinking about sound rather than interpretation. You do want to have a quality that brings the listener in, but if there's no variation and it's all of the same emotional depth, a song becomes boring. When I discussed how to break the lyric down in chapter 3, I showed you how to deliver a better understanding of what a song is about. There are beats, breaths, and new intentions behind each chorus. Sadness has many colors, not just a cry. It has anger, confusion, surrender, detachment—all these different emotional levels are present when one experiences a loss. So when you sing the song, make sure it's not monotone and that it has dynamics. You must draw your listeners in and take them with you. I personally like voices that have textures that aren't always perfect, and you can hear the change of thought in the voice. Just as when you converse, there's a natural swing to your vocal pattern, with different levels of highs and lows.

Another thing to think about is how famous singers perform other artists' hit songs. They interpret the song while still sounding like themselves. It's the quirky vocal nuances and phrasing of Reba McEntire that make her popular, the vocal transparent airiness of John Mayer that's undeniably his, and the gritty raw bends and squeals of Steven Tyler that belong only to him. None of these artists would change their style or voice to imitate the original singer. I would recognize Rod Stewart's rasp anywhere, even when he's singing jazz standards. If your voice sounds too much like the original artist's, you become a vocal chameleon. You should perhaps get a job in Vegas as an impersonator, or do session and jingle work, because you are not truly developing yourself as an original artist. The balance is to have that recognizable sound and honor what you are singing by making us believe you.

DESIGNING A CANVAS OF SOUND. Creating a canvas of sound for your music is something to consider as well. Think of bands like U2, The Beatles, and Coldplay for starters. Each band has a definite canvas of sound. You can recognize their signature sound through instrumentation, musical production, and vocals. It's the sonic blend of all these three elements voice that sets each of them apart. The Beatles experimented with orchestral strings, horns, and great vocal harmonies to create their distinct signature and style. U2's sound is distinguished by Bono's emotional voice, Edge's guitar, and the ambience and floating feeling in the music. Coldplay features Chris Martin's angelic tone, acoustic upright piano, ethereal and lush rock guitars, and percussive beats to create their vibe. Hence, instrumentation and the blending of the voice are essential.

YOU AND YOUR BAND. A band is there to support you and your songs. Ninety-nine percent of the time, I cannot hear the lead singer when I listen to other bands. And I think that many band members are not even listening to each other. Hearing a solid wall of sound makes people tune out. I always have my students practice with the lights out, and facing each other. If they can't hear the words of the song, or each other's individual parts, they are too loud and have to turn down and start all over again. This should be done until the levels are perfect. If that doesn't work, they then practice the songs unplugged or acoustically until all the levels are right. This is really when the listening starts. Don't kid yourself, major acts practice for months at a time before heading out on tour, and the more experienced musicians know that they are a part of a musical collaboration, and are not the soloist. Everyone's part adds to a song. Here again, layering and textures, fills and musical transitions, all play a big part. It is imperative to listen to each other and together develop your musical dynamics as a unit. I suggest analyzing one of your favorite recordings of your musical genre, and try to replicate it live. Use its production as a study. What is happening in the song instrumentally from the verse to the chorus to the bridge? At what point in the song does each instrument come in? Where does the layering and buildup begin? Where are the transitions, crescendos, breakdowns, and repeated musical hook lines/motifs? Apply these same concepts to your production, and practice until you are able to embellish your songs with your own approach.

Reviewing How to Develop Your Sound

1. Develop your vocal texture and find your golden tones.
2. Choose the right songs, in the right key, for you.
3. Create a canvas of sound instrumentally.
4. Combine and layer your instrumentation during rehearsals.
5. Try playing songs unplugged, adding ethnic or rare instruments, with the full band.
6. Use productions of other songs as work samples.

9

TECHNICALLY SPEAKING

THINGS EVERY SINGER SHOULD KNOW

"The musician who always plays on the same string is laughed at."
—Horace

Much of what I was discussing in chapter 8 addresses the marriage between the technical and the aesthetic elements that can enhance your sound, such as spending time in the studio with the right producer, learning about musical effects and gear, and understanding what the best way is to get a good sound during live a performance. In this chapter, I will address topics that you will absolutely need to know if you take your show live or on tour. On the DVD in the part pertaining to this chapter, I will walk the stage, identify equipment, and demonstrate various mic techniques and sound effects.

> Do you know about your microphone?
> Do you know your sound terminology?
> Do you know the difference between stage monitors and
>   the house mains?
> Do you know how to set up your show and your backline?
> Do you know about playback tracks?
> Are you knowledgeable about gear (ear monitors, instruments,
>   amplifiers, what cables and extra gear you need to bring)?

TESTING, TESTING, 1-2-3. Here's something that amazes me. Do you know anything about microphones? You probably spend more time deciding what kind of coffee you want at Starbucks. A microphone is what all singers use, and most of them use the one they are handed at a gig. Can you imagine your guitarist, keyboard player, bass player, drummer—anyone in your band—using blindly what is handed to them, having no knowledge of how it works? Can you imagine not knowing the difference between weighted and nonweighted keys, or the kind of pedal effects that could be used, or the cymbals and drumheads available—as if there were no other options out there? I suggest that whatever instrument you play that you research and learn everything you can about it, and about which one is best and affordable for you. Have you ever tried singing into different microphones to see which is best for your voice, or researched an artist with a similar voice texture to yours to find out what type of microphone they use on live tours? I didn't. I know we all can't afford equipment endorsed by the famous, but we can learn about our what our top choices are and find some at consumer prices, and thus gain knowledge about what to look for in a microphone. I'm not an accomplished audio engineer, nor do I pretend to be. I have a Pro Tools LE system in my studio and have learned over the years about sound and gained some basic technical knowledge that I'd like to share with you. But let's talk to a professional who has much more knowledge in this area: David Pearlman, who builds, designs, and manufactures his own line of studio microphones, Pearlman Microphones. They are amazing, by the way, and my cowriter and producer, Dean Landon, and I have used them for years now, along with other Pearlman clients including Miley Cyrus, Jesse McCartney, Annie Di Franco, Dr. John, Black Eyed Peas, Josh Grobin, and many more. Dave's also an accomplished musician, a brilliant guitarist, with years of touring experience, and an amazing producer and engineer. If anyone knows his stuff, Pearlman does. We sat down to talk about voice textures and a little bit more about sound and microphones.

© ARVDIX

Q: Dave, can you educate us a little bit on microphones for live gigs in general. And keep it in simple terms so that we nongeniuses can understand. What's the best microphone for live performance?

A: Especially for live sound reinforcement, you want to go with a really super-high-quality dynamic microphone. [Shure's] SM58 is the best microphone in the universe for live club work, because it is indestructible. It is always going to work. They take superhigh sound-pressure levels and they sound great all the time. There are also certain companies, like Sennheiser, that make both dynamic and condenser live mics, and Neumann, which makes phantom-powered condenser stage microphones that are super reliable and have a better frequency response than an SM58. And don't forget Electro-Voice also makes great stage mics.

Q: What's the difference between a dynamic microphone and a condenser microphone?

A: A dynamic microphone will take a much higher sound-pressure level, but it will not react as quickly as a condenser microphone to change your frequency, because of the acoustics and the physics of the dynamic microphone. You'll get a better frequency response with a condenser.

So Dave is saying a condenser microphone tends to be a bit more sensitive and if you use one they require something called phantom power. So make sure to tell the sound person that you will need phantom power at your shows.

Q: Tell us more about condenser vs. dynamic; does it make a difference depending on the kind of voice a singer has? Which one is good for which type of voice?

A: Every microphone has its own application, and every microphone is going to sound different. So if you have a really high voice, you're not going to want a microphone that is going to accentuate high-end frequencies. It might become a little irritating. You're going to want a microphone that's going to be accentuating more lows and make your voice sound a little smoother. You might want to go for a tube microphone (as opposed to a transistorized microphone) that will sound a little harsher.

Q: Do they have tube microphones for live performance?

A: Yes, there are tube microphones. But it's kind of rare, because tube microphones tend to be a little more fragile. Now, when you are talking about a tube live microphone, there are no handheld tube live mics. It is going to be a fixed microphone on a stand, so it's still going to be a studio microphone and maybe not really matter in a live situation. If you are a jazz Diana Krall type of artist and you want the smoother vibe, a tube might be more appropriate if you're looking for that kind of thing. If you're in a rock 'n' roll type of situation, a dynamic mic or a transistor microphone is more rugged. A tube microphone, you're not going to want to throw around like Roger Daltry. You're not going to want to smash it on the ground. But you will get a smoother sound out of it.

Q: Most people don't know they can test microphones. Where can they do this, and why is this important?

A: I tell people this all the time. They are always saying, What's the difference between your microphone and this mic? Why should I buy a dynamic mic, why should I buy a condenser mic, why should I buy a ribbon mic? And I tell them most cities have a rental place where you can go and rent three or four microphones and take them to your own venue. Because you're only going to be able to tell, in your own venue, if it's going to work for you. You can go to Guitar Center and say "test, test, check, check, hey 1, 2," and see what you like. But if this is going to be the microphone you take to all your gigs, you could also rent four or five mics and take them and sing with them before choosing. If you're doing a bunch of live venues where you need to know you're going to have a consistent sound from venue to venue, I'm not being paid by Shure, but I say take an SM58 or use it as a backup microphone in a live situation.

There's a great story about Roger Daltry. Shure had made I think, their millionth SM58, and they were going to present Roger with the actual millionth mic. All the executives were there, and the first thing Roger did with the mic was to raise it over his head and slam it onto the ground.

Q: Why!?

A: Because that's what always happened to his mics. Roger Daltry is the lead singer of The Who, but some of you youngsters might not know this. Roger would swing the microphone around and spin it, and every once in awhile the cord would get loose and the microphone would smash onto the stage. And he'd pick it up and sing into it, and it would still work. So when he slammed it onto the stage at the Shure ceremony, all the executives were like "OH!" and he picked it up, plugged it in, and it worked. And that's why you should carry an SM58—it's rugged and reliable when all else fails.

Q: This is a little off the subject, but a singer-songwriter comes in to your studio, and they have an idea in their mind of a certain kind of style and sound they want to create as an artist. What is it that makes someone's voice stand out from the rest? Is it microphones, or production, or effects?

A: When I work as an engineer and someone steps in front of the microphone, the one thing I'm looking for is talent. You're laughing, but it's the truth. At one of my last sessions, a prominent songwriter and producer came into my studio. A girl was brought in to sing a song and copy the track of another woman who had, in my opinion, already done an amazing vocal. I knew the original singer, and said, "Why not just clean up this original track and use it?" And they said, "Well, she's not as pretty as this new girl. We need a girl who's prettier to do the video, and sing the song, and this is the artist we want to push." The new girl had all this plastic surgery, but didn't have the innate talent that the other woman had. I was told to open 30 tracks in Protools for the new singer. And we did 30 different takes of this girl singing the song. She left, and the producers said to me, "Okay, let's hear the first word of the first track." And I said, "I'm not your guy—I can't do this. You have a perfectly wonderful vocal from the original artist." They went and found somebody else to do it, and assembled 30 tracks splitting words and syllables, pitch-correcting each and every one of them, and eventually created a vocal track. I'm looking for somebody who can sing. I'm looking for emotion and articulation and someone who can put a song over. They have pitch, they have a great quality, and they can do a take and I can say, "We got it!"

The Singer and The Sound Engineer

THE SOUND ENGINEER IS YOUR BEST FRIEND. When you are gigging, remember that your soundperson can be either your best friend or your worst enemy. The production crew is often overworked and treated poorly. I always bring a gift, a cookie, or a drink—anything to let them know I appreciate what they do. Having good people skills equals getting good treatment. But keep in mind that some local pubs have crappy sound systems, so the more you know, the better you are. Having said that, having knowledge in this area is important. Knowing what it is you're looking for will help you ask for the sound you want. When you're performing in a live venue, there are effects that are created and controlled by an effects send on the mixing board that your soundperson is running. How much of this is used is preferential to the type and style of music, as well as the venue you are performing in. Below, I'll talk about volume, reverb, digital delay, EQ, and compression.

VOLUME (DB= DECIBEL). The volume is the level of sound, measured in decibels, that allows your sound engineer to monitor how loud or soft your voice is in the mix.

REVERB. Natural reverb is the result of reflections from sound bouncing off surrounding walls or objects. I'm sure you've heard it when singing in a cathedral, or a bathroom, or a dance hall with lots of mirrors. This effect can be adjusted by the sound engineer during a live performance, with the help of analog outboard equipment connected to the analog console or with plug-ins from a digital console. Too much reverb effect makes the voice *wet* and undefined sounding, making it hard for the audience to hear the true color and character of your voice, not to mention understanding what you are saying. And equally, if there's not enough reverb, your vocal can be *dry* sounding without effects.

DIGITAL DELAY. More commonly known as *delay*, this is one of the oldest special effects in existence. Delay is different from reverb. A digital delay works by repeating a specific sound multiple times, thereby extending the time of the repeated sounds. Example: $1 - 1 - 1 - 1, 2 - 2 - 2 - 2 \ldots$ (I personally call it the boxing-ring-announcer voice: "Ladies and Gentleman *gentleman gentleman.*") Sometimes when a soundperson gets happy fingers and puts too much echo effect on your voice, you will need to ask him or her to reduce the effect.

EQ. Short for "equalization," EQ is the measurement of frequency. This is the element that the soundperson uses to adjust frequencies to optimize the tone characteristics of your voice.

HIGH FREQUENCY. Electric guitars are examples of instruments with high-end frequencies. You can adjust the high EQ during a practice on your vocal. Too much gain may feed back and will be very bright.

MID FREQUENCIES. These are the standard (typical) range of frequencies that we hear; the natural frequency range of the human voice consists of mid frequencies. Too much mid frequency results in a megaphone sound.

LOW FREQUENCIES. Although necessary for warmth and fullness, low frequencies can cause low-end rumble and muddy and boomy feedback if one is not careful.

So much of what sounds good comes with having a good ear and knowing your music. If your voice sounds too bright (too many highs), mega-phone-like (too many mids), or too boomy (too much bass), ask your sound-person to roll off on either treble, mids, or bass a bit. I also suggest learning by singing with an amplifier or mixing console that has high, mid, and low EQ. Experiment with the levels until you get more educated and familiar with what you like, and what is best for your tone of voice. And if you have a great sound at a gig, ask the sound engineer how they dialed in to your voice. Of course, every room you perform in will be different, but having a starting point is useful. You could take a picture of the mix of your vocal on the mixing board or console, and try it at your next gig. Another great resource is, when you're recording, to ask a good producer/engineer in the studio how they dialed in to your voice and if they can give you any sugges-tions on how to EQ your voice.

keep hand off of microphone head and below red line

FEEDBACK. We've all heard feedback: often we are jolted by a terrible squeak and we in-stinctively cover our ears, crinkle our faces, and cringe a bit. It usually happens when you least expect it and occurs if you hold the microphone too high, cupping the head, or the ball portion of the microphone, or you point it at the stage monitors (see the subsec-tion "Stage Monitors Versus House Speak-ers," below). Sometimes a sophisticated soundperson can dial in to that frequency, if the feedback is occurring too often. But it's up to you to control how you handle the microphone onstage.

Monitoring Your Self and Your Stage

EAR MONITORS.® Today, most artists performing on television and in con-certs wear "ear monitors." They can be a lifesaver and are an investment worth making! Now they even come in colors—anything to make them cool and hip. Christina Aguilera has rhinestones on hers. They are custom-molded earplugs with a body-pack receiver and rackmountable transmitter, allowing the lead singer to hear his or her vocals and play back directly instead of through the stage monitors. Stage monitors have been used for years, but the more you gig, the more you'll realize how often you still can't hear yourself. So singers end up pushing their vocals to the point of losing their voice, and thus singing off pitch. With ear monitors® you will always hear yourself clearly. Sometimes your experience of being in the room is muted a bit, and wearing them takes some getting used to. I usually take one of the earpieces out so I can hear the buzz of the room, and leave one in to hear my vocal. Everyone is different. You'll need to visit an audiologist to get earmolds made as well as purchase the body pack and transmitter. I have been using Future Sonics ear monitors® for years, and they are awesome. Take a look.

STAGE MONITORS VERSUS HOUSE SPEAKERS. An option to inear monitors are stage monitors, two large wedge speakers on the stage floor in front of you. They are where you can hear the sound of yourself and your band. Depending on the size of the stage, I usually have only my vocals and the keys playing back from the stage monitors; this is because the stage is often small, the guitar and bass amps are blaring in both my ears, and the kick drum is shaking the floor. The one thing you can almost always count on is the inability to hear your vocal. So crank it up. On a larger stage, if you are farther away from each other, you'll want more of the band mixed into your monitors to feel the music.

MONITOR ENGINEER VERSUS HOUSE SOUND ENGINEER. In larger venues, another thing that is essential to know is the difference between the monitor engineer and the house sound engineer. Now that you know the stage monitors enable you and your band to hear yourselves, there is also an engineer usually to your right side-stage handling the levels of your stage monitors. He or she is a completely different engineer from the main house sound engineer mixing the sound for your audience to hear. There's a mixing console that is usually toward the back of the room you are performing in, and another mixing console off to the side of the stage. When you need stage-monitor levels adjusted, you ask your stage-monitor mixer, not the house mixer.

MONITOR ENGINEER (MIXER). This is usually the person sitting behind the console to the right of you, side stage. He or she handles your onstage playback levels in your stage monitors for you and your band members.

SOUND ENGINEER (MIXER). This is usually the person sitting behind the console in rear area of audience. He or she handles the mix for the house or for the audience to hear.

WHAT YOU HEAR ONSTAGE IS DIFFERENT THAN WHAT THE ROOM HEARS. So now that you realize there are two different audio streams that exist, don't base your show on your stage sound. When hearing both the stage mix (from your stage monitors) and the house mix (playing out for the audience), there often is a bit of latency or time delay. If there is a soundcheck, have the soundperson turn off the house speakers and listen to just the stage mix to help adjust for levels. Then he can bring the house mix back up. I also always get off the stage and listen from the front of the house to make sure the balance is good. Have your guitar player or background vocalist sing in the lead microphone to measure whether all your levels are good. Also, always make sure during a soundcheck to play the loudest as well as the softest parts of the song to see if you can hear yourself. I will make one important note: the sound will change once the seats are filled. After some time on the live circuit, you'll get better at knowing what works for you. At some point having your own personal sound engineer can be a huge safety net!

Backups Just In Case

BACKING TRACKS. When you begin gigging and touring, the pressure to sound exactly like your CD is high. So much can be done in the studio that is often difficult to replicate live on stage. In that event, many artists have backing tracks they sing or play along with live: a mix of the song is made, without the essential parts that will be played live. Lead and backup vocals, guitar parts, bass parts, drums, and so on are performed on an instrumental/click track.

Your drummer has a copy of this mix, often in an MP3 WAV or AIFF format, with the click track panned hard right and the musical track panned left. You'll need either an iPod or a laptop to playback MP3, WAV, or AIFF file, and for playback, with a stereo one-eighth-inch (1/8-inch) headphone jack to a one-quarter-inch (1/4-inch) cable (pictured above) connected to a 4- to-8-channel submixer (channels may vary). Other cables may be necessary, depending on the unit playing the music back and the submixer being used (pictured below.)

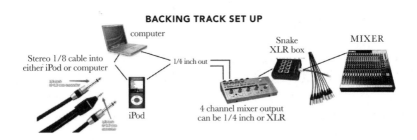

BACKING TRACK SET UP

computer

Stereo 1/8 cable into
either iPod or computer

1/4 inch out

Snake
XLR box

MIXER

iPod

4 channel mixer output
can be 1/4 inch or XLR

And the 4-channel submixer, 1/4-inch cable, or XLR will need to be patched through a snake XLR and into the house mains and playback monitors. The drummer hears the click track in his left ear, the song mix in his right ear, and usually has eight clicks or a 2-bar lead-in to count the band off. Everyone then comes in and plays along to the track. An MP3 player or a laptop is good because they rarely skip. Just make sure that your drummer puts whatever medium you're using (iPod or laptop) on a pillow somewhere, so that the kick drum doesn't bounce it around. When your playback track skips, it can be a nightmare.

WHAT IS A BACKLINE? A backline is the musical equipment you will be using and/or bringing to the event, including any specialties required by the venue; some venues have a permanent drum kit, keyboard, and/or bass amplifier. Usually bass heads, guitar amps, and keys are brought by the band. You can ask the venue what they provide and tell them what you need. Microphone stands and mic cables are sometimes provided by the venue, but if you have a large band and lots of singers, you may want to inquire if they the house has enough of them to go around. There are two ways to provide venues with your backline information—by giving them either a stage plot or an equipment list.

A stage plot allows the venue to see where you like your bandmates positioned onstage. Note: you always talk about right- and left- and up- and downstage from the performers' perspective, not the audience's.

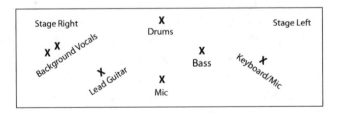

A list will do just as well, and you can pick your places during sound-check once you get there:

> Lead vox (vocal)
> Electric guitar
> Electric bass
> Keyboard/mic (boom mic stand for keyboard)
> Background vocals (BG vox): 2 mics/2 straight stands

*If an acoustic guitar is in your band, ask the venue if they provide a

DI box, which will allow the acoustic guitar to be directed through the main house speakers as opposed to having to plug into an acoustic amplifier onstage.

SOME MUSICIANS LIKE SPECIFIC GEAR. If the venue is providing you with the backline, that is the equipment that's already at the club, so make sure it's compatible with your show. The following details should be discussed with your band members:

> Keyboard model
> Type of amplifier being provided for the guitar and bass players
> Brand of cymbals and snare for the drummer

When you become big and famous, on tour you'll also get a rider tray. This has all the food and drinks you want backstage. You've heard stories of famous stars only wanting white m & m's on their rider trays. That's what it is!

Emergency Kit

Always have bags with extra cables, footpedals, batteries, and backup equipment in case something breaks down. I performed on a Circle Line cruiser around Manhattan, New York. We were playing to backing tracks, and we forgot one power chord. So for two hours on a Friday night party cruise liner we had to improvise, and performed an acoustic set. We were able to make up for it, but it was not what they expected of us. Had we had an emergency kit, the problem could have been resolved. I also personalize my cables and footpedals, and all my equipment has my name on it, with colored tape around each piece, so the production crew doesn't keep it when breaking down for the next act.

These seem like simple things you should know. But how could you know, unless you've gigged or toured a lot. Now you'll know what to ask for and what to call things, so that when you're touring the circuit you won't be labeled as a "chick singer" or a "naïve rocker dude."

I cannot reiterate this enough: Excessive loud volume can lead to tinnitus and hearing loss. Take caution when playing live, use earplugs, and purchase ear monitors® if you gig a lot.

PART III

LIGHTS, CAMERA, ACTION!

10

THE CAMERA VERSUS THE STAGE

BIG OR SMALL OR NO ONE AT ALL

"All the world's a stage."
—William Shakespeare

My first national television experience was one that I would not want to relive. Although everyone watching who didn't know me may not have known any difference, I felt like a deer in headlights. Today, with cameras and playback so easily accessible, you can film your performance prior to your debut and tweak a few things in your favor and learn how to avoid problems.

I had been performing a lot, so my nerves did not normally kick in anymore. But this was a first time on television, a million people watching, and a couple of factors played a huge role in my performance. The camera visually adds ten pounds to one's appearance on screen, and it emphasizes all of your features. If you've ever seen a live-theater performance and then met the actors following the show backstage, their makeup is extremely dramatic—shadows and highlights are almost clownlike. Their movements and expressions onstage are exaggerated, so that they can be seen by the entire audience.

Film and TV are the exact opposite. The smallest raise of an eyebrow or other facial movement speaks volumes. So again, know yourself and your features, and you're halfway there. Let's go all the way back to my standup world. This is a direct result of being the world's biggest mugger. To begin with, I have large features and a big personality, so television only enhances that. I had a stage coach explain to me that the camera would basically be focusing on the upper portion of my body. There would be a few long shots, but mostly quick cuts and angles of my face and shoulders. So we spent a lot of time in the mirror working on upper body movements and interpreting my song physically. Right before I went onstage, I was told, "No matter what, don't forget to really open up your eyes." I did open them, and I looked like Lucille Ball after being caught by Ricky in a racket of some sort.

You must consider how exaggerated you will look once you're filmed. If you frown too much, open your mouth too wide, or show a broad range of emotions, it is magnified. You don't want to be Jim Carrey—and I love this guy, but not for what we do. At the same time you also don't want to look dead, or Botoxed, and emotionless. So, you must find the middle ground.

Usually, three cameras focus in on you. In some cases, a live audience is in the room as well. Whom do you perform to in this case? Both, actually. First, I always think of the camera as another person in the room. So it is another member of the audience. Staring it down and performing only for that one person is awkward. The camera represents the people at home who are watching you and getting uneasy sitting in their living room thinking, "What is this person doing?" And you've suddenly become an amateur like that guy jumping up and down and yelling " Hi Mom!" during a live shot on the news.

I say, pretend the camera is a friend in the audience. You can glance across the audience with a sparkle in your eye and let people at home feel as though they are watching you in person, along with everybody else who is actually there. But look past the camera, slightly to the right or left of it, as if you're talking to someone standing next to it, so that your body language is open and the audience can see what you're feeling. (Celine Dion addresses the camera directly. Some performers do, and it's a personal choice. I've always been told not to look into the lens of the camera.)

In a live television shoot, there are a few things you should know. You get to run the song before the studio audience is brought in, because the crew needs to check the sound and do a test run with the cameras before the actual filming. So ask the production team to let you rehearse during the sound check exactly the way they will be filming it once the studio audience is seated. In my rehearsal the house lights were off, and I was staring out into a dark abyss singing to my imaginary friends. Once I went out to sing for the real take, the audience had been all pumped up by the warm-up comedian, and the entire house was brightly lit. The audience was seated in bleachers, and I was being stared down by huge smiling faces and excited fans who were in Hollywood watching a TV show! It was super high energy that I played up to, and very unexpected. Hence, an over-the-top look. (So again, make sure to request that they rehearse with all the lighting set exactly the way it will be for the actual shoot.)

The multiple-camera setup is a method of shooting for television. Several cameras are placed on set, and they record the show simultaneously. When the show is being recorded live, the director is in the control room editing what the viewer at home sees. There are generally three types of shots.

LONG SHOT. These shots are of all, or nearly all, of the band, with large parts of the stage and showing groups of people in the audience.

MEDIUM SHOT. These shots show a person from the knees or the waste up, with medium-size groups of people in the audience.

CLOSE-UP. These shots show the head, neck, and shoulders of a person; facial expression is very important.

Each camera will have a red light that goes on to let you know when you are being filmed. This can be distracting. I suggest that you pay no attention and instead let the crew do what they do best. There's no need to play to the camera. The idea is to be in the room, but be aware that the audience at home is getting a supersize version of your face. So the more relaxed you are, the better you will come across. Try not to think about the millions tuning in, and do your best to perform for both.

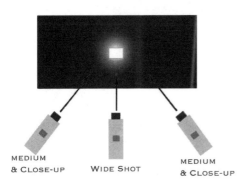

MEDIUM
& CLOSE-UP   WIDE SHOT   MEDIUM
& CLOSE-UP

Especially when you are performing in a live-filmed show, refer back to chapter 3, in which I talk about breaking down the lyrics and interpreting a song. Think about your facial expressions and how they are imparting the meaning of the song. Also, remember it doesn't have to feel good to look good, and it doesn't always look good when it feels good. The example I use for this concept is to remember a party you went to and you were having a blast! In fact, way too much fun and a friend took your picture. You felt great, but the photograph is horrendous. Your face is all contorted and the picture is way too close! That's something to think about when performing on camera as well. I will reemphasize the importance of practicing and filming and watching the playback. This way you can take a mental photograph of what it feels like physically when you achieve your best look. Practice this over and over again. Models do this all the time. They know their best side, their best angle, what colors are flattering, how to hold their hands, position their legs, how wide to smile, and so on. Soon it will become more natural, and you as a performer can avoid many of the mistakes others made before you. You will also get better and better at it. The key to being seasoned is just that—years of experience and of perfecting your craft.

11

THE INTERVIEW

TIPS ON HOW TO KEEP US TUNED IN

"If every word I said could make you laugh, I'd talk forever."
—UNKNOWN

These days, most musicians are not invited to talk after performing on television shows. Is this because many musicians are not good interviewees? Or there is a preconceived notion that musicians are not always the sharpest tools in the shed? I hope to dispel that preconception. I know many brilliant musicians, and I know that today's music industry is promoted primarily through visual media such as television shows, YouTube, iTunes, cell phones, MTV, and VH1—all of which bring audiences directly into the lives of artists. We've become a reality-based population. And it's nice to get to know a little about the artists behind the music. Who are they? Why did they write their songs? What are their interests, hopes, and dreams, and how can their musical expression become important for a greater cause? Furthermore, with concert ticket prices becoming more and more astronomical, today most will likely tune in to a show to get a closer look at their favorite singer. Sadly, this is where some musicians fall short. Expressing themselves through music and lyric is often seamless, whereas the art of speaking suddenly invites odd pauses, lots of *ummm*'s, *yeah*'s, *like*'s, or just dead airtime.

It used to be that you attained instant stardom if Johnny Carson invited you over to the couch after a performance. If you were able to sing and be interviewed, then you were a cut above the rest. Today, you're lucky if David Letterman walks over and shakes your hand after you perform. Still, no interview follows even that accolade. So why not raise the bar and have a regular segment on talk shows when musical guests are also interviewed.

When appearing on a television show, you will want to know what is expected of you and how you can wow your audience. There are many things veterans know that first-timers do not, and this chapter will focus on the tools and preparation you'll need in order to give a great interview. It will give you a peek behind the scenes.

Before reviewing what I've collected over the years, I want to give you a chance to hear some great advice from a true professional, Jane Velez-Mitchell. She hosts her own show, *Issues with Jane-Velez Mitchell*, on HLN Headline News, a more news-driven media show. She has, however, been on *Celebrity Justice, Larry King Live,* and *The View* and has served as news anchor in both New York and Los Angeles for years. In her work she has interviewed thousands of celebrities, and has herself been interviewed as a celebrity guest. She is someone who has firsthand experience from both sides of the desk, and she is the perfect person to share some inside advice on preparing for an interview.

Q: What interested you in becoming a journalist?

A: I got interviewed on television a couple of times and that peaked my interest. I originally wanted to be a syndicated columnist who would type out my opinions, and I decided that since I had been interviewed on television I would check out broadcast journalism. As to why I wanted to be in journalism, it was pretty much I think because my father and I would always debate the news. It's what I was accustomed to growing up. And I was very opinionated. I had strong opinions about everything. Those opinions have changed over the years. I was very interested in politics, so it seemed a natural fit to do something that I was so interested in. I would probably do it for free, and I have done it free several times, but somebody was willing to pay me for it, so I decided to get involved and followed my passion. You have to be passionate about something to be successful in it.

Q: So now that you have your own show and have been on television for 32 years, how do you feel audiences have changed? What do you think today's audiences are looking for?

A: I think they are a lot more sophisticated. You can't just be a big pho-ny-baloney and pull the wool over their eyes anymore. They know when somebody is not being real. And they have so many more options, and they can reject you very quickly. It's not like the old days, where there were three channels. Now there are millions of Internet sites and hundreds and hundreds of channels, so they have a lot of opportunity to make a different selection. There's not a second to waste; you've got to really tune in with everything you've got.

Q: That leads me right to my next question. Technology is aggressively changing the way we communicate. There's so much information that we can access by just the flip of a button. It's harder to stand out among all the traffic. Do you have any advice on how to be memorable when you're being interviewed?

A: I think that to be original and be who you really are is the key. Not to imitate anyone. When I first started I didn't know what it was like to be an anchor, so I imitated other anchors and, consequently, I was phony. As one news director put it, I reeked of insincerity. And then over the course of doing therapy and a lot of other things like self-analysis and self-development, I figured out more about myself and was able to finally relax and be that person. That's what people want—they don't want a cardboard cutout of somebody else who's successful doing the same thing you are. Originality, that's what they want—something fresh, something original, and, of course, something valuable. If you're singing off-key, it doesn't matter how original you are, unless you're Andy Kaufman or perhaps Tiny Tim. Maybe in that weird sense you can be off-key. Kaufman, in particular, made it by really being off-the-charts original. But I think people want something new, something different—they don't want the same "old." Authenticity and originality and someone who has the courage of their convictions—and they're not just going to be timid about what they're offering. And you could be somewhat controversial in the world of infotainment and entertainment. Bring something to the table—be unique, unique, unique.

Q: What do you expect from an invited guest on the show? What does a host want from a guest?

A: Different shows want different things. Letterman would want you to be funny and clever, and what we look for is someone who is articulate, high energy, and has an opinion. It depends on what venue. Mostly, I want a point of view.

Q: Do you give them questions?

A: No, but I expect my guest to do their research and know what we are talking about. It's very obvious when they haven't. So do your research and know what you are going to talk about.

Q: What advice do you have for someone when they hit a blank wall and can't think of what to say?

A: You should always have something else to say. The main mistake people make is they get wrapped up in their own ego. Yeah, sure you've got to look good; you've got to have your makeup and hair done. But then you've got to let go of that and realize that you've got to be of service to the viewer. The most important thing is not to be ego based. If you're ego based doing what you're doing, I don't care what it is—performing or talking on television or doing an interview—if your ego is at stake, you're going to be fear based. And when you're fear based, you're not your best self—you're often your worst self. My main suggestion to people is to realize you are there to do people a service of some kind; if it's entertainment, then entertain. If you're a comedian, make people laugh. If you're a singer, give people something beautiful to hear. If you're a newscaster, give people information. If you're a host have a point of view and give people something to think about. You're there doing a service. You're not thinking about yourself. That's the most important thing, to let it go. It's not about you; it's about being a conduit for something more.

Q: Any dos and don'ts or quick tips?
A: Don't be phony. Don't be rabidly self-promotional, like artificially mentioning things you're trying to hawk. You've got to weave those in. And the main thing is, hopefully, you're providing something that is life-positive. Another thing to know is that you're going to make mistakes. Don't let them totally throw you. When you make a mistake, you get up and brush yourself off and continue on. Sometimes you're going to make a fool of yourself—it comes with the territory if you are a performer. You are going to have a pratfall one time or another, and the main thing is to keep on going and not let it throw you emotionally and psychologically. It's easier to do that if you regard it all as an adventure and fun, and then you won't be ego-driven or motivated or fear based! If you're not having fun with it, no one else is having fun with it. A career shouldn't be a cause for agony or sleepless nights. It should be fun. I look at my career as I'm doing this now: it's not going to last forever, and it's an adventure.

Hopefully, Jane has helped you by giving you a little look into her world and the media. Following are some additional tips that I've learned along the way.

ALWAYS HAVE A CLEAR OBJECTIVE. Think about the press junkets that actors have to go on to promote a movie. They are asked the same questions over and over again about their new project. Have some information that you want to share with the audience about your new project, and weave it into your conversation and find creative ways to talk about it in your interview.

The idea is to know what you want your audience to get from your appearance. Do you want them to

> Buy your new CD?
> Attend an upcoming concert?
> Donate money to a cause?
> See the movie that your song is in?
> Learn more about the process and passion behind you recording
> your latest project?

Be precise and clear as to what you want your audiences to know.

PRACTICE ANSWERING QUESTIONS. Prepare some questions and practice answering them aloud. It does not have to be exact every time and try to keep it natural, but it will help you break through the habit of using *uh* and *like* to fill in the blanks! And always have something in your back pocket if the interview is not going well—something you know will revive the energy and story line. Perhaps a funny story, something related to what you are talking about. Often the interviewer may say, Anything else you'd like us to know? Practice something clever and fun, or a callback. A *callback* is what comedians use when referring back to the first punch line of their show. It's almost a full-circle moment. For example, if the famous animal advocate Jack Hanna were the guest before you, and he'd had Mookah the Monkey crawling on Ellen DeGeneres's head and messing with her hair, when it's time for you to come out you might say, "Ellen, I was thinking you and Mookah, you might consider him for your hairstylist." You break the ice, open up a laugh, and set up a comfortable, fun vibe. At the end of the interview, you could say, "And if you download my new single, you can get a free hair consultation from Mookah!"—a great closer, and people will remember you.

BE ENTHUSIASTIC ABOUT THE SUBJECT. Most people are moved and remember someone's passion more than what he or she specifically says. Be yourself and rely on the strong points of your own personality. Don't forget that television enhances everything: facial expressions, body language, energy, posture, attitude, and what are called *unspoken cues*. Watch the delivery of other guests on shows, and you'll see how much they accentuate what they say with unspoken cues. If possible, take a brisk walk before going on camera to get your blood flowing and wake yourself up.

DON'T LEAD ME OFF THE BEATEN PATH. Don't allow the interviewer to sidetrack you. I always have a way of answering a question and pointing the conversation into the direction I intended. For example, if someone were to ask me, "You grew up in Texas. Tell us about your childhood," I would answer, "That'll take an entire year and an antidepressant, but what I do want to tell you is . . ." (fill in whatever it is you want to talk about). You never want to say no to the interviewer; instead, you want to lead them somewhere else. As you can see, I use humor a lot—you may not. Find your strength in language and personality, and use that.

BRIEF ANSWERS ARE THE KEY. Simple and sweet is the key. Communicate everything you need to in the first 30 seconds, and don't give every detail leading up to the event. Tell your audience exactly what you want them to know in an entertaining way. Also try using a sound byte: compose a few lines that sum up what you are trying to get across to the audience. Think of commercial jingles or slogans as examples. Practice writing a few that are visual and catchy. (For example, I used to say that my CD *On Gardner Street* was about the many faces of love.)

IF YOU HIT A DEAD ZONE, REPEAT THE QUESTION. If you are not sure about an answer, repeat the question before responding in order to buy time and to focus.

KNOW WHERE TO LOOK. Think of the camera as invisible. You would not be looking away from the person talking to you. So keep a strong eye contact with the interviewer. Shifty eyes often give off a sense of uneasiness and a lack of authenticity. Be "in the moment" and let the audience experience that with you. If there is an audience in the room, you might look out and address them when appropriate. Also, if you're seated, do not slouch in the chair; sit up and lean forward—it imparts interest and excitement.

USE POWERFUL LANGUAGE/MEMORABLE PHRASES. There should be a sense of urgency in your language that will show how excited you are about your project and the buzz it is generating. If you are promoting a new CD or a show you will be performing in, mention it by name.

MAKEUP. The camera lights are very, very hot. If a makeup person is not provided and there are no options, apply translucent powder (sample) before going on TV, or you will look shiny, oily, and plastic. Matte makeup and contouring makes you look the best for the camera. Still, I think it's a must to hire a makeup artist if one is not provided. If money is an issue, you can visit a local makeup store (Bloomingdale's, Macy's, Sephora, or Mac) and have one of the makeup artists in the store help you.

APPEARANCE. However you decide to dress should be paired with the impression that you are trying to make on the audience. If it's a serious topic, such as a fund-raiser to raise money for a disaster, dress simply with solid colors and earth tones. Or if you want to be taken seriously, dress in a sophisticated and sleek fashion. If you want to have fun and purely entertain, wear something colorful, bold, and playful.

BE FLEXIBLE. Anything can happen on TV, so you need to remain calm, confident, and flexible in case the unexpected happens. The audience will laugh with you if you are relaxed and in the moment when a goof-up occurs.

Sample Interview Questions

- How has music changed your life?
- When did you realize that you were going to be an artist?
- How old were you when you first started to sing?
- Were you raised in a musical environment?
- What other talents do you have? If you hadn't pursued music, what career would you have chosen instead?
- What's on your music playlist that we would never think would be?
- What's one of your most embarrassing moments that you're willing to share?
- What has been your proudest moment so far?
- What would people be surprised to learn about you?
- Who are your heroes?
- What's been your toughest obstacle?

SWITCHING SIDES. Ask a friend to interview you, and videotape the interview. Try switching sides, and you ask the questions. There is something very valuable in knowing what it's like to be the one conducting the interview. Both roles have their challenges.

In this chapter, I have discussed ways to create a memorable interview. Remember, you will not have enough time to say everything you want. Be selective, concise, and entertaining. Future interviews will provide opportunities to add other nuggets of information. The best advice in the meantime is to use your personality strengths and express the passion you are feeling, thereby making your first interview an unforgettable one.

PART IV

THE INDUSTRY

12

BEHIND THE DESK

AN A&R'S TAKE ON IT ALL

"Let the music play on, play on play on"
—FROM LIONEL RICHIE'S "ALL NIGHT LONG"

I don't know about you, but I always feel intimidated and scared by industry representatives. Meeting them is like going to the principal's office: you'll either get advanced to the next grade or expelled. Many idolize or vilify them. The music business is a big business, and any big business is about the bottom line—making money. There will always be competition and oftentimes corruption. The question you're all asking might be, how and when did art equal commerce? In the '90s, much like Wall Street today and our current economy, the consolidation of record labels and multi-billion-dollar companies with shareholders demanding a quick growth on their investment all led to the downfall of the industry. The get-rich-quick strategy destroyed labels and the potential careers of thousands of artists. Nurturing the musicians and developing their talent took too much time, and that practice was soon eliminated. In today's music world, for example, artists such as the Rolling Stones, U2, and Bruce Springsteen would not have been given the opportunity to grow and evolve into some of the greatest rock bands of our time. They would have fallen by the wayside, because a new model to turn a profit would give budding artists only six weeks from the release of their debut CD to getting a radio hit and video rotation on MTV. All the legendary bands took years to develop. And then the Internet opened up a whole new world for the consumer. Some find this paradigm shift to be a better one; others still yearn for the earlier days, which they feel resulted in a better product. Today's music artists have more outlets and are able to choose whether to direct their career with a label or without one. In this regard, the control has been given back to the artist. Still, without the record industry, we wouldn't have our favorite stars, and without us the industry never would have existed.

Because the industry has changed drastically, I have interviewed two music executives who are artist friendly and from different generations to discuss the good old days, today's market, and what's to come. They are not the CEOs of the record companies; rather, they are the ones who stick their necks out for the artists they believe in. What is it that interests them in becoming the music gurus behind the scenes? Like the great and powerful Wizard of Oz, once they step out from behind the curtain and their façade is broken, A&R reps, managers, and music supervisors are just people, doing what they love. We have a passion about writing and performing, and they have a passion about discovering, developing, and supporting talent.

First, I spoke to Don Grierson, who has seen it all and has been in the music industry for 40 years. He's the legendary A&R executive who came from Down Under, where he got his start as a disc jockey at the age of 17. He rose to prominence in the recording industry, discovering and working with many of the most notable artists of the late 20th century, including Heart, Joe Cocker, Celine Dion, Tina Turner, Bad English, Cyndi Lauper, Duran Duran, Gloria Estefan, Cheap Trick, Little River Band, Kenny Rogers, and Anne Murray, to name a few. He was even involved promotionally with the launching of the Beatles' label, Apple Records. He got me my record deal, is a lifelong friend, and makes a mean margarita. He is now a consultant to artists and works independently.

Q: You have the nickname Golden Ears. Who gave you that name?

A: I guess when you've been around doing what I've done for so long and you have a little bit of success, people think you have good ears. It's not legendary—it's just been attached to me somehow.

Q: You have worked with some of the biggest artists in showbiz through your career, and you found some hit songs for artists and paired them with writers. Can you tell us about one or two of those?

A: Philosophically, there has always been one key to the success of this business. If you are a singer—whatever genre of music—in order to reach a broad audience (as opposed to a niche market like heavy metal, or jazz, or dark blues), the key for a singer—whether they write songs or get them from another source—is to find hits. I've always believed firmly that an okay singer can have success, at least in the short term, if they have a great song.

But I also believe, on the other hand, that a great singer is not necessarily going to have a lot of success if they have mediocre songs. So to me the magic, and when it happens it is magical, is when you have a great singer or someone who is able to communicate vocally and they find the perfect song. If they don't have a song, therein lies the challenge. A lot of artists write their own material, and there's nothing wrong with that, except sometimes artist think they write great songs when they don't. And many who have had success with songs they have written, sometimes creatively dry up, and they don't write hits any more. They blame everybody but themselves; they blame the label, the promotions department, but really the problem is the missing link, the song.

Over my career I've had the opportunity to work with some amazing singers. Some of them were self-contained, and others were great singers but needed material. I worked with Anne Murray, an amazing vocalist. She's been around for years and years, sold millions of albums, and she didn't write any of her songs. When I was at Epic and I signed Celine Dion, she too was another great vocalist, but not a songwriter. In those cases, you're going to the songwriting, publishing community looking for great songs, and that is the challenge. On the other hand, you have an artist like Heart, who I signed when I was at Capitol. Heart had been on Epic Records and had some big singles and albums. Ann Wilson, the lead singer, is an amazing vocalist, and Nancy Wilson's a great guitar player and singer in her own right. The band had an identity and a history, but they stopped writing hit songs and they were not looking at themselves, but looking at other people. I remember sitting with them before I signed them. I thought this is an amazing talent, a unique act of two sisters with a great image; everything was in place except songs. They said, "We're writing," I said, "Great." Now this is where the ability to create a relationship with the artist is very important. I said, "What happens if you don't write a hit? You're looking at me as a partner. I'm your A&R person, so we're in this together. You must respect my opinion, and I will respect yours. That's why I'm here. Would you be open to doing some cowriting?" They agreed. We put them together with other writers. I also said, "If we get lucky with a song from the outside community, would you be willing to do an outside song?" And begrudgingly they said yes. I put the word out to all the writers and publishers to find them a gem or two, just in case they didn't come up with some hits. They themselves didn't write a single; they did, however, cowrite with an outside writer and wrote "Never," which eventually became a top single— but still we didn't have enough for an album. We found four outside songs that became giant successes: we had a No. 1 single with "These Dreams," two Top 10 singles with "What About Love" and "Nothing at All," and a Top 30 single with "If Looks Could Kill." And from selling 200,000 albums on Epic, they were now selling millions on Capitol. The key was that the talent was there; what they didn't have were songs. Ron Neverson came in as the producer, the songs were added, all the pieces fit, and when they brought in the music to Capitol, they went nuts! "Oh my god—we've got smashes here." That first album is now close to selling 10 million units. They went on from there to having great albums with outside writers Diane Warren (Celine Dion, Cher, Aerosmith), Mutt Lang (Def Leopard, Shania Twain), and even Billy Steinberg (Madonna, Pretenders). I love this group. And while both Anne and Nancy Wilson are amazing, they haven't written a hit single since the Epic days. If you have the singer, you need the song. Everybody has to do his or her job well in order to have success. I believe that will apply no matter what day or what the technology—the basics are the natural human connection. You can be trendy and have moments, but I'm talking about songs that last, songs that create careers, songs that give you a long-term run.

Q: Who would you say had that it factor, that total stage presence, that blew you away?
A: I got to work with Joe Cocker, who I signed to Capitol. He had the "it" factor, or rather the Cocker factor, there's "magic" on the man. He is a rock 'n' roll legend. He had a lot of problems with drugs and booze, which he admits, and he has said, "I should have been a statistic." He really shouldn't have survived, with the lifestyle he was living. But he is perhaps, to me, the most soulful artist I ever worked with. He is a true artist in the sense he sings from the heart. He had a single called "Civilized Man," and they wanted a music video for it. So the company put together a video team, and wanted to keep it really honest, not something trendy. It was going to be shot in black and white and appear to be of a soundcheck in a club. The camera would shoot through the chairs on the tables, and the band would be on the stage doing a soundcheck. It was a really down-home, basic type of video, with close-ups of Joe singing. Well, I'm at the Capitol Tower, and I get a call from the producer saying, "We've got a problem with Joe." And I'm thinking, don't tell me he slipped off the wagon, because he was having problems at the time. The producer said, "The problem is Joe can't lip-synch." I said, "What?" The director explained, "He doesn't know how to lip-synch." I asked to speak to Joe, and I said, "What do you mean you can't lip-synch?" He responded, "They want me to sing it exactly as it is on the tape. And the thing is, I recorded that vocal a few times in the studio. I

sang it differently every time. And the producer did some editing, putting things together. I sing from my heart—I can't sing it exactly as it is on the tape. The producer did that, not me." I thought, "God I've never heard this before. How more honest can you be?" So, we got a backing track for Joe, and he sang live while filming his music video. His vocal is a live take. Now that's a true artist. Later, he had to learn to lip-synch. I thought, How more true an artist can you be? That was Joe. He's the most sincere, soulful artist that I've met. Then working with Tina Turner, a gem and a class act, and even Bob Seeger, and incredible people like that. They're all unique, and they are just amazingly talented. When you have that luxury like I did, you think to yourself, Who's looking down on me, how did I get so lucky?

Q: Did they have good work ethics?

A: Most real artists do. They may have their moments if they are into drugs and alcohol. Heart was never a problem, neither was Tina. Joe had drug problems, but he worked through them. There are always teen-type artists, who probably think they're more important then they are, and act accordingly. And the real artists will be difficult at times; it comes with the territory. But they're fighting for their being; they want to do it their way. They need help sometimes, but most of the time they just need a little focusing. I found most of them to be totally professional. Don't forget they're artists; you're not going to expect them to say, "Yes sir, no sir."

Q: Compared to the artists that you've worked with in the past, how does the industry affect the up-and-coming artist?

A: There is a definite difference, because the [type of] artist we've been talking about was the [in the] heyday of the music business, as we know it. That was the time of the CD. They were booming and you sold big numbers. That was before the Internet. The majors controlled the industry, they had the money, they had major artists, they had the budgets, they controlled radio, retail, and MTV, and in fact they controlled everything. There was a funnel, which was the world of A&R. We were the people, right or wrong, good or bad, who said yes and no to artists. And we'd make decisions and we would be right or wrong. But, other than getting in through that filter, so to speak, there really was no other way to break into the mainstream industry, with rare exceptions. Today, however, with the Internet as powerful as it is, artists don't have to go through that system anymore. The major labels found out music was being downloaded for free, and people weren't buying CDs anymore. And with stealing and iTunes coming into the world, you didn't need an album; you could just buy a track you liked, if you were willing to pay. The majors' profit margins were drastically cut. They weren't selling the volumes of CDs or albums anymore; they didn't have the power. Towers and Virgin Records are all gone, retail is scattered at best, the box stores (like Wal-Mart, Best Buy, and Target and occasional small stores like Amoeba) sell CDs, but they're rare. Most of music sales now are happening online. Today's artists going for the mainstream are under enormous pressure to have hits. It's a real singles business. The majors are the only ones who can chase the pop hits [by people like] like Lady Gaga, Britney Spears, and Bruno Mars. Those majors are the only ones who can afford artists like this; they're looking for the quick hit and hope to sell a lot of albums, which doesn't often happen. You may get a Taylor Swift selling 3 million albums and a Lady Gaga, who is proving to be a viable album artist, selling 4 million. But, if they'd had those success stories back before the Internet, they would be selling 10 to 15 million albums. You can imagine, that's a big difference in profit margin. Today, the pressure is on record labels to get a hit single immediately, and they don't do what they used to do—allow artists to develop. That takes time. But if you develop an artist, it will give them time to grow, and you'll find out their strengths and weaknesses. You really believe that the talent is there, but you know they aren't ready yet. Today the pressure, due to economics of the business and our society, is to get immediacy. You can't develop an artist and have immediacy at the same time. So they don't have artist development, and young artists need that. It takes time and the labels are not doing it, so it's hard [for new artists] to find their way into the major system.

But, on the other hand, artists can do it themselves. Many prefer this; they don't trust the labels and the accounting and the 360 deals in place, and often artists are being charged back for everything. So many will do it on their own. But the difference is when the label signs you, they are taking the risk; when you are doing it, you're taking the risk—it's your money. Still, you don't have to sell the big numbers to pay any kind of big money back to the record company. I still believe very firmly that the public—whether they buy it or steal it, and people don't steal what they don't like—still wants artists who are fresh and unique, talented, and have great songs. When that happens, boom! Success comes.

Q: To an artist today what would you say still holds value, regardless of change?
A: I think an artist has to define who they are and what they want to be. And they should have a center. If they don't, they are throwing themselves in the mob, so to speak. You may have a quick moment of fame, a cool little thing

on YouTube, and lots of hits. There have always been one-hit wonders—a quick hit and then they disappear—because there was no substance there even before the Internet. Those who believe they are true artists must build around a center and in the mix, perform live, create an image for themselves without gimmicks, so you have a look. But, you must have material and songs that will resonate with an audience. No one can say what will and won't resonate with an audience, but you can try to eliminate the ones that don't, judging by history, and knowledge, and gut instincts. If you have the songs, you can compete. Then how you get them in front of an audience is the challenge. That has always been a challenge. If you've got something of substance, you now have a chance.

Q: Do you believe the substance has diminished over time?

A: Yes, because we've gotten away from the developmental elements of what artists usually need. If you look at history, for most of the great artists who had long-term careers, big catalogues, and who are still working, it didn't happen quickly. They grew, they were given time. Bono said if they had been signed today in this climate, they would have been dropped because they didn't sell any albums in the beginning. Most of those acts didn't, and they were allowed to grow. The Police, when they first came over here, they were a white reggae band and everybody was saying, "What is this?" And they played in clubs for 30 or 40 people. But labels believed in the potential, and the artists were given time. Chris Blackwell, who started Island Records, signed Bob Marley when no one wanted to, and later signed U2. When he first heard U2 he said, "I didn't like their music at all. It did nothing for me. But when I met them, I knew I had to sign them. They were determined, focused, and they knew where they were going." They are one of the world's greatest bands today. That is the true record guy. He signed them based on his gut. Because they had it, and he gave them time. If that happened today, the A&R guy would get kicked out.

Q: What would you say to an artist starting out?

A: Get your sh-- together. Define who you are. Do you want to be famous? That's not going to work. How serious are you about the craft? Are you willing to work, practice, and go out and slug it out, get kicked, and get knocked down? Are you willing to do it? Because if you're not, it's not going to work. You have to be willing to put yourself on the line, believe in yourself, and continue to hone your craft. You should work with people who can help you, not hurt you, creatively. Get the best possible songs with melodies. Classical music was not about vocals; it's about melodies and it stood the test of time. That's never changed. Melody is still the key: a chorus, a hook, and lyrics that fit. Without the melody nobody cares. Focus on the basics. If there are two people in the audience, give them 110 percent. Maybe next time they bring five people. And you build, and you build, and you build, and when it's tough you slug it out. That's what all the great artists do, and have done. You practice 10,000 hours. You do the hard work that it takes. Most people will never have success in five minutes. And if you think it's going to come on a silver platter, it won't. And if you think you deserve it because you think you're great, you're not going to get it either. Because you have to earn it; you've got to make the audience want to see you again. That's how you build a career. And you have to be serious about it—it's not a game, it is a business. It's simply music and business. But as I've always said, "Without the music, there is no business."

Don is a man with years of experience, and someone I always turn to when I need advice. It seems that a lot of the artist development these days is going to be happening on our own time. I work with students, day in and out, helping them discover what type of artist it is they really want to be. I ask them what is their plan of action. Many say, "I don't know. I'm an artist and I simply want to sing, write, and express myself and not be so concerned with all the rest." To which I'll answer, "You don't have to do anything, but you might as well bury your head in the sand." Of course it's hard to take everything creative and put it in a box. Nobody wants to do that, nobody is asking for that. But, you have to have a clear vision. And don't feel labeled, because over time it may change. We all grow and branch out over the course of a career. Take Pink or Queen Latifah: both started out in R&B and rap, and look where they are today. Even Gwen Stefani, who started with the ska band No Doubt, moved from there to her solo career, and Sting, originally with his band, The Police, evolved musically into a jazz-infused pop, and now, with his latest CD, is singing with a full orchestra. They've all evolved over the years, and we've grown with them. But when they launched onto the scene, there was no question about who they said they were. They are artists whose attitude, commitment, and intensity shine through. So as you break into this world of entertainment, infotainment, tweets, YouTube and iTunes, the more centered and focused you are, the better you will be.

I also sat down with Richard "Rico" Csabai to talk about how labels are handling music and artists today. He is currently an A&R manager for Rick Rubin's American Recordings in Los Angeles. It's an independent label with a smaller artist roster including the Avett Brothers, Johnny Cash, ZZ Top, and Slayer to start. In addition, Csabai is the cofounder and owner of Intelligent Noise Records and Management. Previously, he held positions in both A&R and publicity at Island Def Jam Music Group.

Q: Rico, you spend so much time celebrating art and music and discovering talent. You can change someone's entire destiny, and that often goes unnoticed. You must love music. Are you a musician?

A: Yes, I have played music since I was a child. My parents made all the children in the family take piano lessons at a young age. My mother at one time was an opera singer as well, so our whole family grew up with a great appreciation for music and the arts.

Q: How did you become involved with the record industry?

A: I got my first real start interning at Island Records, which ultimately led to a job there. Previously, I had been in bands and done some touring. Almost always I would act as the manager for every one of them, which taught me invaluable lessons.

Q: Who's your favorite artist of all you've worked with?

A: It's impossible to pick just one, but certainly one that means a lot to me is Slayer. I've been a fan since I was a teenager, and it's kind of amazing to end up working with them years later.

Q: What was it that Slayer did that you feel stood out? Was it their workmanship, their songwriting, their shows? Did you learn anything from working with them?

A: They have never sacrificed an ounce of artistic integrity throughout their career. Their fans are the most loyal of any band I've ever seen, because Slayer has always delivered great albums and live shows. Working with them has taught me how important it is to respect your fans.

Q: Most people are unaware of the pressures that A&R reps have in trying to find the next "big" thing. They too can get dropped from the label, so A&R reps have the same demands on them as the talent does. I hear songs all the time and see so many performers that are great! How do you pick and choose and recognize the ones who are a cut above the rest? When did you know you had a special quality in spotting talent?

A: There is a certain feeling you get when seeing another person perform who is simply a star. Most of the time you're seeing things that are good or middle of the road (even a lot of signed artists fall into this category for me). The moment you see or hear someone great, it is undeniable. It hits you in all kinds of ways that nothing else does. Probably in high school is when I realized I had a knack for this. It was a hobby of mine to help put bands together for other musicians, or for my own projects. I was always scouting the best bands in town to perform with and book shows for, as well.

Q: The paradigm shift from the traditional music industry model to a more digitally driven one has affected labels directly. We have a new generation of online consumers. As a result of this, how many new artists are signed yearly?

A: Well, an exact number would be quite tough to quantify, but certainly fewer artists are getting signed to major labels annually compared to a decade ago. When I was first starting out, there were almost too many new artists being signed to even keep up with. Now I would say that's been cut in half. On the bright side, there are more indie- and artist-owned labels than ever before. New artists need to keep in mind that there is never a knight in shining armor to ride in and save the day. No matter how talented you are, you've got to educate yourself about the industry and be just as savvy on the business side of things.

Q: What is considered a success? (I sold 134,000 singles on an indie label, and, sadly, the label folded. To me, that's a lot of records).

A: There are so many new revenue-sharing partnerships (that is, taking a percentage on publishing, touring, merchandise) going on now between labels and artists; record sales alone aren't always an accurate barometer of success. Sometimes a very smart deal, a cheap record and campaign can be a success on 100,000 units or even less. Conservatively, if you can sell 250,000 to 300,000 units, especially as a new artist, that should be a success in some regard.

Q: Now, focusing more on the talent side, what's most important for a developing artist to focus on?

A: Songs, songs, songs! Write as many as possible—I'm talking hundreds. Just because you have written ten songs doesn't mean you should record an album. If you're not a great writer, then find someone who is to write with, or write for you. This still happens at the very highest levels, so don't be afraid to collaborate. Work on your performance, not just by playing shows, but really get creative with how big or small your production might be, what it will consist of, and how you're going to emote your songs to the audience.

Q: Is a great show and demo enough to get signed these days?
A: Technically, yes. I find that happens much less than it used to, except in the pop and R&B world. That still exists to some degree. Most labels are looking for something to build on and take to the next level.

Q: Where is the future of music heading for someone who is trying to make it? If you were an artist, what would you do to get yourself signed?
A: The future is going to be focused on creating and owning a niche. [So I'd say to work on] superserving your fan base, with a focus on touring and providing interesting and creative content at multitiered prices and platforms. If I were an artist, I would be doing the above. Taking the time to build a grass-roots, truly passionate base of fans that will follow you your whole career. If you can do that on a basic level, that means someone can expand your business to a potentially wider audience.

Q: Anything else you'd like to add?
A: Keep it honest. Don't go chasing trends and fads; it's better to start them yourself, instead. Build a culture, not a brand.

In the end it's all about the songs, knowing who you are, and being honest with all the choices you make. This is a small peek inside what is happening on the business end. It was not until I became business savvy and put all the pawns in place myself that something started to happen. Of course, some of it was being in the right place at the right time. But it also had a lot to do with keeping my eyes and ears open, and being aware of how everything works.

PART V

PUTTING IT ALL TOGETHER

13

FOLLOWING YOUR JOURNEY

SUMMING UP

"Your sole contribution to the sum of things is yourself."
—FRANK CRANE

I trust that this book has opened your eyes and provided you with new insights and journeys to take. Whatever it is for you, the most important thing to remember is that you are building a career. There are ebbs and flows in this tepid industry. To make music and make a living as an artist is a blessing. I don't believe we need to be running on a treadmill with a carrot dangling in front of us to make us think we'll never reach that goal. And setting the bar too high will only result in a letdown. I've met many artists who have successful careers gigging at festivals, playing local clubs to sellout crowds, and doing humanitarian work with their music. Ask yourself what it is you want to do with your music? Now that you have a better insight into your role as an artist and the impact you have on people's lives, you might decide that you long to be more than a flash-in-the-pan hit product for a record label. Don't get me wrong—having a huge song on the radio, touring the world, all of the perks that accompany this would be amazing! But fame should not be the driving factor, or the sole reason you choose to pursue a career in music. Those artists selling millions of records are working nonstop; it's a very intense life, and they are constantly under the microscope. When I was signed, it was a mixed blessing. Sure, it gave me validation to say, I did it! But, that's when the real work began, and I had to make the record company feel that it hadn't made a mistake by investing in me. I realized that it was a business deal and had nothing to do with my heart, my soul, or my songs. To look back at my body of work as a songwriter, an artist, and a teacher, the record deal was a small part of it. The beauty of being an artist is the process, the actual creation, the joy you get from doing what you love, and not just its outcome and the accolades. All this is to say, perhaps your goals will change, your opinion about who you are will grow, and new inspiration will come into play. Because there is enough room in this world for you. And I believe it's never too late. Through our music we say, as Karl Paulnack puts it, "I am here; my life has meaning." How you choose to do this is up to you. The doors are wide open.

Taking Notes

Chapter by chapter, I've covered key elements to help you achieve a better understanding of who you are as an artist, and secrets and techniques to strengthen your stage presence and performance. What now? What are your goals? All of these things should be put in order to help you move forward and in the right direction. Take all the art, colors, poetry, mood boards, words, feel sheets, new ideas, and creativity exercises we did and explore. What have you added to your name/persona, setlist and show, fashion ideas and imaging, voice and musical texture, stage presence and interview tips to make a new impression on your future audiences? What exciting new adventures are you about to embark on?

Let's put it all together in this final questionnaire.

1. Mark "Yes" for elements you feel committed about.
2. Mark "No" for areas you are unclear about and revisit those chapters again. (I do believe that ideas also need time to marinate in the subconscious. Perhaps the creative playground you've built will spark new ideas in days to come.)
3. Mark "Needs More Work" for elements you want to continue to develop and any additional notes you want to make to yourself.

Review Questionnaire

1. FINDING YOU

Element 1: Recognizing your on and off switches

Yes   *No*   *Needs More Work*

_____

_____

_____

Element 2: Creating a stage name and musical genre

Yes   *No*   *Needs More Work*

Element 3: Looking at how others may see your essence

Yes   *No*   *Needs More Work*

---

2. CASTING YOURSELF

Element 1: Show style

Yes   *No*   *Needs More Work*

Element 2: Enhancing your personality type

Yes   *No*   *Needs More Work*

Element 3: Applying these elements

Yes   *No*   *Needs More Work*

---

3. YOUR LYRIC IS YOUR CONVERSATION

Element 1: Breaking down lyrics: three points of view

Yes   *No*   *Needs More Work*

Element 2: Positioning each POV body

Yes   *No*   *Needs More Work*

_____

_____

_____

Element 3: The art of practicing

Yes   *No*   *Needs More Work*

_____

_____

_____

4. THREE CHAKRAS

Element 1: Understanding the three energy centers

Yes   *No*   *Needs More Work*

_____

_____

_____

Element 2: Physically using chakras

Yes   *No*   *Needs More Work*

_____

_____

_____

Element 3: The art of practicing

Yes   *No*   *Needs More Work*

_____

_____

_____

5: DESIGNING YOUR SET

Element 1: Creating a theme

Yes   *No*   *Needs More Work*

_____

_____

_____

Element 2: Choosing your songs

Yes *No* *Needs More Work*

_____

_____

_____

Element 3: Creating a show on and off stage

Yes *No* *Needs More Work*

_____

_____

_____

6: BETWEEN THE MUSIC

Element 1: Using stories and anecdote

Yes *No* *Needs More Work*

_____

_____

_____

Element 2: Making better transitions

Yes *No* *Needs More Work*

_____

_____

_____

Element 3: Leaving the audience wanting more

Yes *No* *Needs More Work*

_____

_____

_____

7: THE LOOK

Element 1: Learning the basic no-no's

Yes *No* *Needs More Work*

_____

_____

_____

Element 2: Creating a feel sheet

Yes   *No*   *Needs More Work*

_____

_____

_____

Element 3: Shopping in your closet

Yes   *No*   *Needs More Work*

_____

_____

_____

8: SONIC SOUND

Element 1: Working with new instrumentation

Yes   *No*   *Needs More Work*

_____

_____

_____

Element 2: Finding your golden notes

Yes   *No*   *Needs More Work*

_____

_____

_____

Element 3: Rehearsing the band

Yes   *No*   *Needs More Work*

_____

_____

_____

9: TECHNICALLY SPEAKING

Element 1: Understanding microphones

Yes   *No*   *Needs More Work*

_____

_____

_____

Element 2: Talking to your sound engineer

Yes   *No*   *Needs More Work*

_____

_____

_____

Element 3: Knowing the stage and gear

Yes   *No*   *Needs More Work*

_____

_____

_____

10: THE CAMERA VERSUS THE STAGE

Element 1: Performing for the camera

Yes   *No*   *Needs More Work*

_____

_____

_____

Element 2: Understanding camera angles

Yes   *No*   *Needs More Work*

_____

_____

_____

Element 3: Tackling both live and taped performances

Yes   *No*   *Needs More Work*

_____

_____

_____

11: THE INTERVIEW

Element 1: Defining the interview goal

Yes   *No*   *Needs More Work*

_____

_____

_____

Element 2: Using personality strengths

    Yes   *No*   *Needs More Work*

_____

_____

_____

Element 3: Understanding conversation techniques

    Yes   *No*   *Needs More Work*

_____

_____

_____

ACKNOWLEDGMENTS

This book is a labor of love, and could not have happened without the support and assistance of so many. I would like first to thank John Cerullo for making the publication of this book possible. Thank you Marybeth Keating and the editorial staff at Hal Leonard for all your hard work and support. Thank you Ana Esteves for your assistance, friendship, and enthusiasm. Special thanks to all the interviewees for your participation and dedicating your time and expertise including: Grammy nominated engineer Dave Pearlman, the infamous Martha Velez, golden ears Don Grierson, new additions Cat Winnekamp, Manuel Benecides, Rico Csabai, and a special thank you to my aunt Jane Velez-Mitchell who has been both a role model and a cherished friend.

Thank you to my many teachers, mentors, and musical colleagues; to my father Maurice Peress who gave me the gift and love of music, my brother Paul Peress for being my very first band mate and co-writer, my mother Gloria Vando for your love, your words and hours of listening, my sister Lorca Peress for letting me spread my wings to compose for theater, to my other father Bill Hickok for always believing in me, and my grandmother Anita Velez-Mitchell for passing down all your secrets to life and show-biz. To my vocal and performance coaches: Dan Zollars, Dorothy Hall, Steven Memel, and Toni Basil for all you've taught me. To my extended family, Nicole, Teresa, Len, Lillian, Chris, John, Delbi, Lynn, Donna, Bonnie, Scott, Darren, Piper, Melissa, Kimberly, and Ross, thank you. Thanks to Leanna Conley and Lisa Tygier Diamond for your contribution in art and photography. An extended thanks to Musicians Institute and all who participated in the making of the accompanying DVD. Musical Guests: Danny Byrne, Josh Misko, Ipo Pharr, Ashley Nicole, Natalie Metcalf, and Taps Mugaduza. Your talent and presence continues to inspire me. Special thanks to Director Zachary Rockwood, Andy Patch, Jordan Hood-Taylor,

Sandra Mohr, and Noah Berlow. And an extra special thanks to my amazing co-writer, producer, and partner in life, Dean Landon, for your constant support and love, I could not have done any of this without you.

You have all been instrumental in my career and life experiences, and your connection with me has contributed to my growth as a person, singer, and performer, all lending to the writing of this book. I can't thank you enough, and I am truly grateful to have been given the opportunity to take this journey.

APPENDIX A

TAKING YOUR PERSONALITY TEST

Please follow this page step by step to take the test, understand it, and learn about your results on the websites provided.

1. Log on to the Internet and visit www.humanmetrics.com. You will see on the upper left-hand side Jung Typology Test, Jung Career Indicator (also known as the MBTI, as I've mentioned in the book). Click on the link.

Take the test.

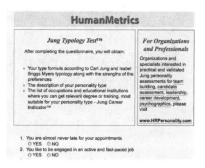

Click on the Score it! tab at the end of the test and find out your "type."

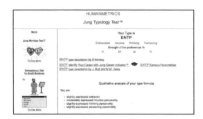

This questionnaire measures your strongest four criteria, and the combination therein leads to career suggestions.

Your type will be a combination four of the eight preferences below that all people can be classified under according to Carl Jung and Isabel Briggs Myers. Your result will be a combination of four letters, which represent the preferences you practice most in life. (There is also a graph provided on page **TK** in chapter 2.)

E = Extraversion	I = Introversion
S = Sensing	N = Intuition
T = Thinking	F = Feeling
J = Judging	P = Perceiving

2. Once you get your results, I highly recommend visiting the link http://similarminds.com/personality_types.html to read about your type. Click on Personality Types.

Choose your type and review.

3. Then, I highly recommend visiting the link www.personalitypage.com to understand more about what the Four Preferences mean.

Click on maroon icon box at the bottom of the page, to the left of "What are Personality Types," as shown below.

Then look up your result on Information About Personality Types. Click on Four Preferences.

There are also Four Temperaments that each type falls under: Guardian, Artisan, Idealist, and Rational. These four temperaments are *"based on two basic dimensions of human behavior: our communication and our action, our words and our deeds, or, simply, what we say and what we do."*

4. I highly recommend visiting the link www.keirsey.com, clicking on Four Temperaments to learn which one "Your Type" falls under, reading about what it means, and seeing portraits of famous people who share your same results.

APPENDIX B

RECOMMENDED EQUIPMENT LIST AND LINKS

SHURE SM58 MICROPHONE The legendary Shure SM58® vocal microphone is a great live microphone; check out the Beta 58 version as well. Visit www.shure.com.

SHURE WH20 DYNAMIC HEADSET MICROPHONE
The Shure WH20 is a rugged, lightweight, dynamic headset microphone that provides high-quality voice pickup and is hands free. Visit www.shure.com.

MG6PRO™ 13MM EAR MONITORS®
Ear Monitors® are to hear yourself onstage directly, instead of relying on the stage monitors on the floor.
Visit www.futuresonics.com.

LR BRAGGS PARA DI The Para DI is a studio-quality direct box that features a 5-band equalizer and allows control over voicing without sacrificing tone. It is engineered to bring out the best in any pickup.
For more information, visit www.lrbaggs.com.

MARSHALL GUITAR AMPLIFIER

This amplifier is used for electric guitar. There are many to choose from, depending on your budget. For more information, visit www.marshallamps.com.

FENDER BASS AMPLIFIER

This amplifier is used for bass. For more information, visit www.fender.com.

JBL STAGE MONITORS These monitors are located onstage and play back the band and vocalist performance so you can hear what you are doing. They also have a great portable P.A. system. Visit www.jblpro.com.

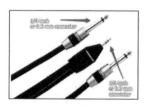

MONSTER CABLES These are ¼-inch cables that connect instruments such as guitars, keyboards, bass, and other electric instruments to amplifiers or to DI boxes going through the mains. Visit www.monstercables.com.

EMERGENCY KITS You should bring an emergency kit with you to every gig just in case the venue does not have the necessary missing component or in case something breaks! Put it all in a duffel bag and have it on hand at all times! Include the following:

XLR CABLES

The cable that connects microphones to the channel strips.

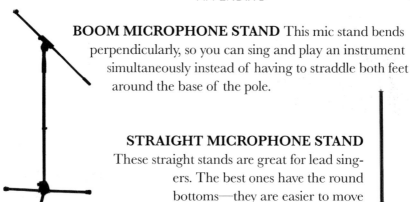

BOOM MICROPHONE STAND This mic stand bends perpendicularly, so you can sing and play an instrument simultaneously instead of having to straddle both feet around the base of the pole.

STRAIGHT MICROPHONE STAND
These straight stands are great for lead singers. The best ones have the round bottoms—they are easier to move around and more stable.

ELECTRONIC MUSICIAN'S EMERGENCY ADAPTER KIT
(These can be purchased)

Power Cables
Universal Sustain Pedal for Keyboard
Guitar and Bass Strings
Guitar Picks
Batteries (Have every kind of battery on hand: D, C, AA, AAA, PP3, and so on.)
Extension Cords
Earplugs
Music Stands
Duct Tape
Throat Coat Tea

INDEX

Adventures of Huckleberry Finn, The, 30

Aerosmith, 70, 116

Akerman, Malin, 72

American Records, 120

Amoeba, 118

Amos, Tori, 57

Anderson, Al, 21

Antioch University, 21

artist development, 22, 119, 147, 118, 120

Auerbach, Red, 53

Authenticity, 8, 18, 108, 105,

Avett Brothers, 121

backing tracks, 93, 95

backline, 59, 85, 94, 95

Bad English, 114

Bad Finger, 49

Ball, Lucille, 100

band member, 14, 16, 17, 28, 54, 73, 78, 83, 92, 95, 101, 115

Barneys New York, 71

Beatles, 17, 54, 78, 83, 114

"Before He Cheats", 48

Benecides, Manuel, 70, 135

Berry, Halle, 21

Best Buy, 8, 108, 118

Beyoncé, 18, 53, 54, 70, 74

Billionaire, 65

Bjork, 73

Blackwell, Chris, 119

Blanks, Jr., Billy, 44

Blanks, Sharon, 44

Bloomingdales, 109

Bono, 75, 83, 119

boom mic, 94, 143

Born Free tour, 54

Boulanger, Nadia, 81

Boston Conservatory, 119

Bowie, David, 15, 69, 70, 73

Callback, 107

Capitol Records, 115

Cardioke, 44

Carey, Mariah, 18, 49, 81

Carrey, Jim, 100

Carson, Johnny, 103

Cash, Johnny, 121

Celebrity Justice, 104

Chakras, vii, 43, 44, 45, 46, 47, 48, 49, 130

Charles, Ray, 63

Cheap Trick, 114

Cher, 15, 71, 116

"Civilized Man", 116

Clapton, Eric, 18, 22, 21

close-up shot, 101
Cobain, Kurt, 43
Cocker, Joe, 18, 114, 116
Coldplay, 17, 83
Compression, 89
Cooper, Alice, 15, 66
Costello, Elvis, 70
Crane, Frank, 127
Crossroads, 71
Crowe, Sheryl ,7, 15
Csabai, Richard "Rico", 120
Cullum, Jamie, 16
Cyrus, Miley, 86

Daltry, Roger, 88
Damian Marley, 75
DeGeneres, Ellen, 107
Dello Russo, Anna, 73
digital delay, 89, 190
Dion, Celine, 18, 70, 81, 100, 114,
    115, 116,
Double Exposure, xi
Dr. John, 16, 56, 70, 83, 86, 103, 121,
Duran Duran, 17, 114
Dylan, Bob, 15, 70

Ear monitors, 85, 91, 92, 93, 95,
    141
Edge 75, 83
Electro-Voice, 87
Elliot, T.S., 69
emergency kit, 142
Enya, 56
Epic Records, 115
EQ, 89, 90, 91
Estefan, Gloria, 114
Expose, 70
fashion spotlights, 69,79
Fender Amps, 142

Fiends and Angels, 21
Fleetwood Mac, 17, 21
Foo Fighters,17, 70
Future Sonics, 92, 141

Gaultier, Jean Paul, 69
Glam Squad, 70
golden ears, 114
golden tones, 82, 84
Google, 74,75
Grammy Awards, 70
Grierson, Don, 114
Grobin, Josh, 86
Gucci, 69
Guinness, Daphne, 73
Guinness Book of World Records, 37
Guitar Center, 88

Hagen, Uta, 23
Hanna, Jack, 107
Hansard, Glen, 15, 76
Heart, 17, 114, 115, 117, 118
heart chakra, 45, 47, 49
Hearst, Lydia, 72
Hendrix, Jimi, 18, 21, 69
High School of Performing Arts, 23
HLN Headline News, 104
Holiday, Jennifer, 7
Hopper, Dennis, 21
Horace, 85

I Am Sasha Fierce tour, 53
"I'm Yours", 49
"If Looks Could Kill", 116
Island Def Jam Music Group, 121
Island Records, 119, 121
iTunes, 103, 117, 120
Jackson, Michael, 15, 22, 29, 54,
    69, 70, 75,

Jackson, Samuel L., 21
Jay-Z, 23
JBL monitors and P.A. system,
   142
John, Elton, 15,70
Jolie, Angelina, 65
Jones, Norah, 7, 16
"Just the Way You Are", 49
Jung, Carl Gustav, 20

Kaufman, Andy, 105
Kid Rock, 54, 70
King, Carol, 15, 81
Klum, Heidi, 77
Krall, Diana, 16, 88

Lady Gaga, 15, 61, 65, 66, 69, 70,
   71, 72, 75, 118
Lambert, Miranda, 76
Landon, Dean, x, 86
Lang, Mutt, 116
Larry King Live, 104
Lauper, Cyndi, 18, 114
Led Zeppelin, 17, 78
Letterman, David, 103
Lighthouse effect, 87
lip-synch, 116, 117
Little River Band, 114
Lloyd, 72
long shot, 99, 101
"Lost Without You", 49
LR Braggs DI Box, 141

Mac, 109
Macy's, 109
Madonna, 15, 69, 71, 73, 116
Marceau, Marcel, 44
Marley, Bob, 20, 21, 119
Mars, Bruno, 49, 65, 72, 75,
118
Marshall Amps, 142
Mayer, John, 15, 56, 83
MBTI's Rationalist, 25, 29, 30, 31
MBTI's Guardian, 25, 29
MBTI's Idealist, 25, 29, 31, 139
MBTI's Artisan, 25, 29,31, 139
McCartney, Jesse, 86
McCartney, Paul, 54
McCoy, Travie,, 65
McEntire, Reba, 83
McLachlan, Sarah, 15, 82
McVie, Christine, 21
medium shot, 101
Megadeth, 56
MGMT, 73
Mime, 44, 46
Mirroring, 5
Mitchell, Mitch, 21
Moneymaker, Kelly, 70, 71
monitor engineer, 92
Monster Cables, 142
Moonwalk, 44
Moore, Julianne, 21
Moore, Shemar, 72
Morissette, Alanis, 15, 82
Mraz, Jason, 15, 49
MTV, 103, 113, 117
Mugler, Thierry, 54
Murray, Anne, 16, 114, 115
Musicians Institute, 135
Myers-Briggs Type Indicator
(MBTI), 20, 23, 24, 137

Nas, 72
Nash, Kate, 72
Neverson, Ron, 116
Nicks, Stevie, 71
"Nothing At All", 116

Oprah, 65

"Paper Doll", 39
Parton, Dolly, 6, 66
Paulnack, Karl, 19, 121, 128
Paves, Ken, 72
Pearlman Microphones, 86
Pearlman, Dave, 86
Peress, Paul, ix
Perry, Katie, 15, 70
Pink, 15, 70, 71, 120
Pink Floyd, 17, 78
Pitt, Brad, 65
Pop Icon type, 14, 15, 18, 27, 29, 31, 53
Police, 119, 120
Pretenders, 116
Prince, 15, 17
Pro Tools, 86, 103
Psychological Types, 20
Pygmalion, 30

Queen Latifah, 120

Reverb, 89, 90
Richter, Johann Paul, 35
Richie, Lionel, 113
rider tray, 95
Rimes, LeAnn, 16
Rogers, Kenny, 16
Rolling Stones, 17
Rubin, Rick, 120

sacral chakra, 45, 47, 48, 49
Sarah and Friends, 53
Seegar, Bob, 117
Sennheiser, 87
Sephora, 108
Seymour, Jane, 70

Shakespeare, William, 13
Shaw, George Bernard, 30
Shure headset, 141
Shure mic, 87, 88, 141
singer-songwriter, xi, 14, 15, 18, 21, 27, 29, 31, 36, 5, 89
Singing with the Great Music Monsters, 21
Sire Records, 21
Slayer Intelligent Noise Records and Management, 121
Sleigh Bells, 72
sound engineer, 89, 90, 91, 92, 93, 133
Spears, Britney, 15 57, 118
Springsteen, Bruce, 15, 113
stage monitors, 59, 85, 91, 92, 93, 142
stage plot, 94
Staples Center, 54
Starbucks, 38,85
Stefani, Gwen, 70,120
Steinberg, Billy, 116
Stewart, Rod, 83
Stone, Joss, 18, 75
straight mic stand 94, 123
Strasberg Institute, 23
Swayze, Patrick, 21
Swift, Taylor, 16

Target, 44, 118
Taylor, James, 15
Tempo, 56, 58
"These Dreams", 115
"The Way You Make Me Feel", 49
Thicke, Robin, 49
third-eye chakra, 45,46,48
This Is It Tour, 54
360 deal, 118
Timberlake, Justin, 70

Tinnitus, 95
Tiny, Tim, 105
Tolstoy, Leo, 3
Tower Records, 118
Tunstall, KT, 15, 58
Turner, Tina, 18, 114, 117
Twain, Mark, 30
Tyler, Steven, 71, 75, 83

Underwood, Carrie, 16, 48, 70

Valentino, Keeley, 39
Velez-Mitchell, Anita, 44
Velez-Mitchell, Jane, 104
Velez, Martha, 20, 21
View, The, 104
VH1, 103
Virgin Records, 118
Vocal Body Movement
    Workshop, 151

The Wailers, 21
Waits, Tom, 76
Wal-Mart, 118
Warren, Diane, 116
"What About Love", 116
Wilson, Ann, 116
Wilson, Nancy, 116
Winnekamp, Cat ,72
Wizard of Oz, 114
www.humanmetrics.com, 24,
    137
www.keirsey.com, 29, 139
www.personalitypage.com, 139

yoga, 44
"You Ought to Know", 48
YouTube, 55, 103, 119, 120
Yustman, Odette, 72

ZZ Top, 121

DVD-ROM TRACK LISTING

1. Introduction
   About this DVD

2. Chapter 3
   Three Points of View: Your Lyric Is Your Conversation

3. Chapter 4
   Using the Chakras: Pairing the Physical and Emotional

4. Chapter 6
   Between the Music: Stories and Anecdotes

5. Chapter 9
   Technically Speaking: Things Every Singer Should Know

6. Part V
   Putting It All Together

This video is available online at
http://makingyourmarkinmusic.halleonardbooks.com.
You can stream the examples online or import all of the full-resolution media
from the DVD-ROM directly into iTunes or any other
full-featured media player for easy playback.